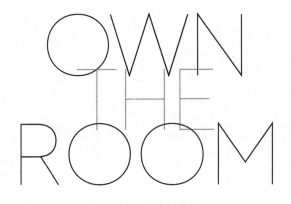

DISCOVER YOUR SIGNATURE VOICE TO
MASTER YOUR LEADERSHIP PRESENCE

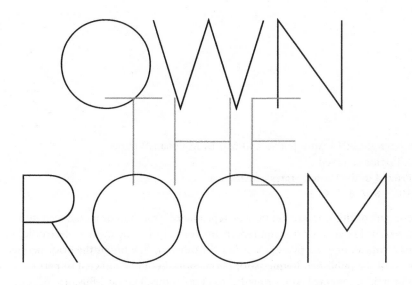

OWN THE ROOM

AMY JEN SU
MURIEL MAIGNAN WILKINS

HARVARD BUSINESS REVIEW PRESS
Boston, Massachusetts

The web addresses referenced in this book were live and correct at the time of
the book's publication but may be subject to change.

Library of Congress Cataloging-in-Publication Data

Su, Amy Jen.
   Own the room : discover your signature voice to master your leadership
presence / Amy Jen Su and Muriel Maignan Wilkins.
      pages cm
   Includes bibliographical references.
   ISBN 978-1-4221-8393-9 (alk. paper)
1. Leadership.   I. Wilkins, Muriel Maignan.   II. Title.
   HD57.7.S82 2013
   658.4'092—dc23

                                                          2012041298

To my parents, Neil and Lilly Jen, for their unconditional love and sacrifices, which have made so much possible in my life. Their imprint has deeply influenced all in my life, including this book.

— Amy Jen Su

To my favorite superheroes—Arden, Noah, and Gabi—for sharing the power of presence with me through their love, laughter, and loyalty.

— Muriel Maignan Wilkins

CONTENTS

ACKNOWLEDGMENTS

We are immensely grateful to a number of individuals, without whom this book would not have come to be. First and foremost, a tremendous thank-you to Amy Gallo, who elegantly played the role of outside editor, relationship counselor, facilitator, reality checker, and friend in the most seamless, gracious way possible. She was indispensable in bringing this book to life. We are fortunate to have worked with our wonderful Harvard Business Press editor, Jeff Kehoe, who helped us shape the ideas and vision we had for this book. His invaluable guidance and continued enthusiasm for the project kept us energized throughout the writing process. We would be remiss not to mention our literary agent, Giles Anderson, who reached out to us after reading our *Harvard Business Review* blog and provided countless pieces of advice as we navigated the book process.

We have amazing coaching clients. Every day we feel honored to work with them and humbled by their commitment to being the best leaders they can be. We are grateful to each of them for sharing their journeys and allowing us into their worlds. They often say that they learn from us, but they are the true teachers. We also thank the sponsors of each of our coaching clients, who provided honest and insightful feedback that helped crystallize the Signature Voice framework, best practices, and tools.

We are grateful to all of the participants in our Signature Voice training programs. Over very short periods of time, they open themselves up to our coaching and feedback and this new way of seeing their leadership presence. We thank them for the honesty and candor they bring to these programs. The anecdotes, questions, and thoughts that they've shared over the years pushed our thinking and deepened our understanding of what it means to have leadership presence.

While we have partnered with many client organizations, there are a few in particular that we need to acknowledge for believing in us and pioneering the Signature Voice training and coaching programs in their organizations: Mary Lyons and the original PRTM team; Katy Strei, Carole Tilmont, and the whole Med-Immune Leadership Development team; Mary Ellen Joyce and Marina Augoustidis at Brookings Executive Education; Keisha Berkely at the National Institutes of Health; the Leadership Development and HR team at Freddie Mac; and Jane Brock-Wilson and the team at Berkshire Partners. A special thank-you to our colleagues and friends Kathy Gallo of the Goodstone Group and Laura Daley, who generously supported us early on to broaden the reach of our Signature Voice work.

This book would not have been possible without the amazing selfless support of the rest of the Isis Associates team. All of our Isis colleagues have touched this project and us in tremendous ways: Pam Krulitz, for her constant willingness to brainstorm and talk about the Signature Voice model and engage in mutual learning; Nina Bowman and Erin McCants Parker, for "drinking the Kool-Aid" and joining the team to support our growth; Amber Romine and Steve Kullback, who demonstrated commitment to learning the ins and outs of the Signature Voice model and facilitating the training at numerous client sessions; Jenny Sheehan, our executive assistant extraordinaire, who always manages to say the right thing and take the right step to create order out of chaos; and to Emily Sopha, our operations manager, who has supported Isis and this book in so many countless ways.

And we thank all of our consulting partners for their tremendous work with all of our clients.

Amy would like to thank some special people who have given meaning to her life and this work: First and foremost, I thank my parents, Neil and Lilly Jen, for their unconditional and selfless support always. Their generosity and kindness has deeply influenced who I am today. Thank you to my husband, Greg, for being my best friend and partner in life. His support has been invaluable to making Isis and this book possible. My son, Jordan, for the inspiration, love, and joy he brings to my life. He motivates me to bring my personal best each day. I am deeply grateful for the community of family and friends in my life. A special callout to my brother Jim and his family, my cousin Emily Lin, and friends Wanda Lin and Pat Gartman, who have not only kept me true to myself but to the original vision of Signature Voice. I am humbled by the group of teachers who have coached me and deeply influenced my approach in this work: Glenn Hartelius, PhD, of Attention Dynamics®; James Flaherty and Sarita Chawla at New Ventures West; and author and coach Barbara Stanny. Finally, to my dear friend and business partner, Muriel Maignan Wilkins, who has been one of my greatest teachers, I am grateful we are walking this journey together. Her remarkable authenticity, entrepreneurial spirit, and drive have made so much of this possible for the Isis team and me.

Muriel would like to thank a few people she is particularly indebted to: First and foremost, I thank God, without whom none of this would have been possible. A heartfelt thank-you to my parents, Camie and Ferauld Maignan, who may have questioned whether I was following the right path but always had the confidence that I'd do the right thing. That confidence brought me a long way. To my sisters, Marie-Jude, Nancy, and Genevieve, without whom I would never have learned to have my own voice. Thanks to each of them for being there no matter what. To my friends Samantha Caruth, Adrienne Lance Lucas, and Kaya Henderson, for the constant source of encouragement. To my business partner, colleague, confidante, and most importantly, dear friend, Amy Jen Su—I couldn't imagine being on this book journey and professional path with anyone else. My twin children, Noah and Gabriela, are a constant source of inspiration, personal growth, and perspective. I learn from them every day. They are my double blessings, and I thank them for always being who they are, unconditional in their love, and so present even on the days when I lose my own presence. Finally, I thank my husband Arden, who has been the biggest believer and motivator of all since day one. His never-faltering encouragement, compassion, loyalty, faith, and love make me grateful to God for him every day.

THE MYTHS OF
LEADERSHIP PRESENCE

D o you know how to fill a room? Can you hold your own and connect with others? Perhaps you've mastered owning the room in your current role, but now, are you ready for the next one? In today's organizations, the demands on managers like you are constantly evolving—promotions, shifting responsibilities, new bosses or team members, an altered industry landscape. And if you don't evolve with them, you will fail to be effective. Yet we have seen many successful leaders wrongly assume they don't have to adapt. They presume that the skills and qualities that enabled previous achievements will ensure they thrive against any and all future challenges. "After all," they say, "isn't this what my success was built on?" But future success is rarely built on the same platform as one's past accomplishments.

All leaders reach points in their careers when what is required to be most effective changes. This means not just changes in the job description or the required tasks but when those around them—the team, the boss, the C-suite—expect something dramatically different. At these moments, your technical skills, no matter how superior, will not be enough. You need to exude leadership presence as well. *Leadership presence is the ability to consistently and clearly articulate your value proposition while influencing and connecting with others.* All technical capabilities being equal, presence is what sets true leaders apart. It enables them to adapt to any situation and connect in a significant way with their key stakeholders, all the while keeping sight of who they are as individuals. When we see our clients operate in that zone—where the substance of skills and the power of presence have come together—we know that they are operating at their best. They have *Signature Voice*: a unique leadership presence that is confident, authentic, and effective across a variety of situations and with diverse audiences. Like a signature, their presence is one that is recognizably unique and leaves a substantive impression on those around them and the organization. It takes this type of presence to own the room.

This book is not just about improving your leadership presence on the surface. It's about taking it deeper and finding your Signature Voice. In its pages, we provide concrete tools and frameworks that accelerate that search and enable you to build on your existing strengths. Given that presence is so important, why is it so difficult to achieve? As executive coaches, we work with exceptionally bright and talented people from Wall Street to consulting firms to biotech companies. Yet many of them don't have a complete understanding of leadership presence. Perhaps you too are confused. Maybe you got feedback that you need to work on your "executive presence." Or possibly you heard one of these things:

"You need to develop stronger presence."

"To get to the next level, you need to enhance your overall presence."

"You don't have a strong enough voice at the table."

"You have great vision, but you need to increase your followership."

"Your performance is admirable, you have deep knowledge about your function, you have a strong work ethic, we value you, *but . . .* "

We've seen how often this imprecise feedback drives individuals to adopt one of two approaches: "I'll fake it until I make it" or "take it or leave it." First, the "I'll fake it until I make it" approach: In the absence of concrete advice, the leader begins to read between the lines and look for quick fixes. He looks around the organization for people who are deemed to have presence and attempts to mimic them. He tries to adopt the same mannerisms, dress, language, and even hobbies. In the end, he acts like someone he is not and loses himself in the process. He works *so* hard to exude presence that it comes off as trying *too* hard and backfires. Others think of him as inauthentic or fake, qualities never ascribed to effective leadership presence.

In the second reaction we see—"take it or leave it"—the individual simply does nothing. This is not because she doesn't want to do something. Rather, the feedback is so nebulous that she is left scratching her head, not knowing *what* to do. If you've received this kind of feedback, you know the quandary: you received strong suggestions to enhance your leadership presence but you have no idea what that means or how to do it.

Obviously neither of these responses is ideal. Individuals feel stuck, demoralized, or like counterfeits. Organizations lose bench strength, fail to build strong leaders, and miss out on opportunities to push to the next level. Without a solid understanding of leadership presence, myths prevail. Leaders adopt a perspective that has been shaped over the years by inaccurate information that ultimately does not serve them well in being effective leaders.

DEBUNKING THE MYTHS OF LEADERSHIP PRESENCE

Below are the three myths about leadership presence that misdirect leaders. These myths are most often perpetuated by their own organizations, and like most myths, are passed down to subsequent generations. Perhaps you've heard or uttered a few yourself.

Myth #1: You Are Who You Are

This is probably the most pernicious myth out there: presence is something that you either have or you don't. You are born with presence; you can't build it. What could be more stifling to development than the notion that you can't attain something no matter how hard you work? Yet we've heard this statement over and over from our clients and from their bosses and even the heads of talent management. Too often people believe presence is something that *other* people have: CEOs, politicians, celebrities, "born leaders." But in reality, there are no exclusive rights to presence. Presence is not just for those who are gregarious or "larger than life." Consider Bill Gates: he certainly isn't the first person you think of when you think "leadership presence." He's not slick, or particularly extroverted, or heavy on the charm. But he has presence in spades. He is highly influential, able to impact others, and true to himself. He has not traded in his trademark sweaters for a polished Madison Avenue suit or his true-to-form spectacles for contact lenses. The power of Bill Gates's presence is that he has laser clarity on his vision, values, and what his contribution is—in the world of personal computers and now in global development. He makes this myth about being born with presence seem irrelevant, even silly.

Sadly, this "you are who you are" myth provides a convenient excuse. It enables leaders to hide behind old habits, function on autopilot, or throw up their hands and say, "This is just who I am." These are not sufficient reasons to dismiss your aspirations to have better leadership presence. In this book, we will show you how *anyone* can have leadership presence if they are willing to do the work.

Myth #2: One Size Fits All

This myth is the opposite of the first, but just as pernicious. Instead of resigning themselves to be who they are and giving up on the prospect of change, leaders try to alter their presence to emulate someone else. They believe they have to look and act a certain way to get promoted or rewarded. Those who try to mimic someone else stifle their own creativity and innovation and fail to build on their own strengths.

This one-type-of-leadership-presence-fits-all approach is wrong. When we work with leaders, we always start with the supposition: *your presence is unique to you.* You can find a presence that lets you be who you are and allows you to make an organizational impact in a way that is distinctly your own.

Myth #3: If It Ain't Broke, Don't Fix It

This myth holds that if you've established your leadership presence, you'll sail through the transitions ahead. Once you've got it, it's yours to keep and there's no need to change or even tweak it. But in reality an effective leadership presence is dynamic. When you progress to higher levels of an organization, what is expected of you changes. Your presence is no exception. Being conscious of where you are in your career and in your organization's pipeline is paramount to ensuring you adapt your presence accordingly.

Over the years, we've found that one of the toughest transitions facing our clients is becoming an officer of the firm. In an enterprise organization, this is when an individual moves from the realm of a single function and takes on the role of an enterprise leader. In a professional services firm, this is the transition from being principal to a firm partner and equity owner. It is one of the most significant, distinct, and difficult transitions that leaders face. It requires quantum shifts in knowledge and perspective, networks and relationships. It demands a vast expansion of one's leadership presence. Yet time and time again, we meet the principal who can't quite grasp the difference between an effective presence as a principal and what's required of her as a partner to influence others—or the functional executive who doesn't see the need to expand his organizational visibility and communication beyond his immediate function. Refusing to appreciate how dynamic presence is can stall even the most brilliant career.

This book provides direct antidotes to these debilitating myths. We talk specifically about the critical career transitions from functional to enterprisewide responsibilities that require a shift in leadership presence and many of our stories focus on people at these inflection points. But because it's never too early to start preparing for transitions, the advice and examples in this book are relevant to anyone, at any career stage.

A NEW APPROACH TO PRESENCE

Only leaders who are able to leave behind the same old advice are able to make sustainable breakthroughs with positive results. Instead of trying to mimic those at the top or doing nothing at all, you need to ask yourself far more fundamental questions:

- Who am I, and who do I want to be as a leader in this organization?

- What is my value proposition to this organization?

- What do my stakeholders—direct reports, peers, boss, C-suite—need from me, and how can I deliver?

- How do I impact the business in a way that is authentic to me and resonates with others?

Only by taking a critical approach that involves both introspection and getting feedback from others can you start building the presence that you want and that the organization needs you to have. When we have taken our clients through such a process, they and others around them see a clear, consistent, authentic leadership presence emerge. But before you can begin to answer the above questions, you need to understand what drives presence.

WHAT DRIVES LEADERSHIP PRESENCE?

When we lead executive programs, we start by asking people to think of someone they know who has effective presence. Then we ask them to describe that person's impact. Why do they identify that particular person as having great presence? What are the qualities that he or she exudes? Typically, this is what we hear:

> He sets a vision and inspires action.

> She effortlessly conveys a clear message to multiple audiences.

> He is confident and also knows when to say, "I don't know."

> She's comfortable in her skin.

> He walks the talk.

> She is aware of what others in the organization think and feel.

> He has the ability to be direct in a nonconfrontational way.

> She has grace under pressure.

Then we ask participants to help us dissect the makeup of effective presence. What is it that these selected people do, or don't do, that make us feel they have strong presence? Typically, this is what we hear: *silence.*

A room full of very smart executives quickly and zealously describe what great leadership presence looks like but are then stymied and silenced when asked to identify the drivers of such presence. Presence is one of those things that, when you see it, you know it. But most people have a hard time articulating what exactly creates it. When you watched Oprah at the helm of her wildly successful show, or Steve Jobs delivering news about the latest Apple technology, you knew you were experiencing a presence that was unique and made a difference. But much harder to pinpoint are the mind-sets, behaviors, and actions that these individuals possess—or lack—that grant them the presence of a leader. Even harder is turning the lens on yourself and figuring out what you can do to increase your impact through your presence.

In response to this black hole of practical advice, this book offers a framework that enables anyone to expand his or her leadership presence by taking concrete actions. We disaggregate what leadership presence is and provide a step-by-step approach to developing your own leadership voice.

AN INTEGRATED APPROACH TO PRESENCE: ASSUMPTIONS, COMMUNICATION, ENERGY

Much of what is out in the leadership literature today approaches presence in a narrowly focused way. One of the most popular books, *Leadership Presence: Dramatic Techniques to Reach Out, Motivate, and Inspire,* provides a compelling argument for using acting techniques to help leaders get their messages across with emotion.[1] This book is very original but lacks a clear connection to the business context. It also places a heavy emphasis on the physical aspects of presence, which, as we'll explain, comprise only one piece of the puzzle. *Executive Presence: The Art of Commanding Respect Like a CEO* offers a series of topics as an answer for building executive presence but lacks an overarching framework to hold the pieces together and doesn't provide readers with an integrated, practical approach to developing their presence.[2] *Executive Charisma* proposes an approach to leadership presence from an outside-in perspective, again focusing on the physical aspects.[3]

In our view, an overemphasis on the physical can cause a person to pursue a leadership presence that is inauthentic.

We bring up these books not to disrespect them—on the contrary, we have learned a lot from them—but rather to highlight the difference in our approach. Clearly, a lot has been written on the topic of leadership presence, and we do not claim to have invented the field. But this book is different. The Signature Voice framework offers a new, more comprehensive lens on this well-trodden ground. It presents an integrated way of working on leadership presence that addresses the whole person and leads to sustainable authentic change.

What makes presence is not *just* the clothes you wear, the words you speak, or how you think. Rather, presence requires alignment between your mind, body, and words—to walk the talk, you need a simultaneous focus on all three levers: mental, skill, and physical. Your presence is an interconnected system of your beliefs and assumptions, your communication skills, and your physical energy. You cannot address each separately or you won't see consistent results. Rather, when you work on all three areas in concert you move from having good presence to having Signature Voice.

Think about a leader who has worked hard to hone his public speaking skills, but has neglected to question the assumptions he has made about his senior level audience. Those assumptions are likely to undermine him, making him feel nervous, unsure, and perhaps even small. No matter how well he frames his message or how clearly he organizes his presentation, he will appear incongruent to his audience. The words coming out of his mouth won't match what people experience from his body language. His presence will be diluted as a result.

In this book, we present an integrated approach to help you achieve congruency. Much like an athlete preparing for a competition by training his mind, skill, and body, developing your Signature Voice is based on conditioning your assumptions, your communication strategies, and your energy. We call this ACE conditioning:

The Three Elements of ACE

- *A* stands for the *assumptions* you make and the mind-set you bring to your interactions with others. This is the mental conditioning that helps you develop the right mind-set to put your best presence forward in any given situation. The assumptions we hold form the fabric of our reality: our beliefs about ourselves, about others, and about the situations that surround us. These assumptions are powerful, even—or perhaps especially—when they aren't recognized or spoken aloud. Assumptions have the power to either set you up for success or to undermine your best efforts.

- *C* stands for *communication strategies*—the techniques and tools you use to engage, influence and inspire others. This is the skills training that helps you develop the techniques and tools to say what you mean with confidence and impact. Communication is the most elemental channel through which we engage with others; through communication, we are able to challenge, inspire, collaborate with, and influence others. To quote an old proverb, the same water that floats the boat overturns it—in other words, as much as it supports us, communication can also stand in our way. We fall prey every day to communication failures: forgetting to listen, talking without providing context, sharing the details rather than big picture, undermining our point by saying too much or too little, and talking around an issue rather than to it.

- *E* stands for your *energy*. This is the physical conditioning that helps you manage the impact of your nonverbal cues and emotions on others. Whether or not you choose to acknowledge it, you have a physical presence that telegraphs strong clues and signals to others. When a leader walks the halls of his department frowning, brows furrowed, and eyes to the ground, concern runs through the office as people try to interpret what his body language means. When another laughs as a team member raises a new idea—even though she means it to be encouraging—the team wonders, "Is she taking us seriously?"

The Signature Voice and ACE frameworks provide a way for leaders to move from vague feedback such as "You need to work on your presence" or "You need to make a stronger first impression" to action using a far more concrete definition:

- A Signature Voice is both authentic and adaptive. You must be true to yourself and connect with others. This is the *signature* part.

- A Signature Voice requires using two voices: the ability to demonstrate one's value and distinctiveness and the ability to connect and align with stakeholders. This is the *voice* part.

- To condition presence, you have to focus on your whole self: assumptions, communications, and energy.

THE ORIGIN OF THIS BOOK

When we first began our executive coaching firm, we found that the answer to so many of our clients' developmental needs was to work on their presence. Not because they didn't have it—in fact, many of them had strong presence. But they had not figured out how to take what they had mastered in a previous role and adapt it to the next level of responsibility. They hadn't figured out how to continue to own the room through their career transitions.

Early on in our work, we recognized that there were patterns and commonalities among our clients, particularly a human desire to both have a voice and to connect with others. We saw that the individuals who were able to achieve both of those things had exceptional presence. Over time, based on our observations and analysis with clients, we homed in on the key levers that leaders pull to enhance their presence. This is the origin of the ACE model. We worked with individuals who helped us understand the intricate relationship between mind, skill, and body and what it means to condition for one's personal best. We also worked with executive-level sponsors and stakeholders in coaching and training programs who shared their own practical strategies, tips, and tactics for building presence. What started out as initial hypotheses nine years ago have evolved into a framework and integrated approach that each new client confirms and shapes. Thousands of clients, from high-potential leaders to presidents of organizations, have used the Signature Voice and ACE frameworks to build their presence and have the impact they want.

PLAN OF THE BOOK

The rest of the book provides a roadmap for examining your leadership presence and doing the necessary conditioning to hone and elevate it to your Signature Voice. It has two components: a diagnostic and a customized action plan. In chapter 1, we introduce a key diagnostic tool called the *presence quadrants* to help you more rapidly understand your current leadership presence and how others perceive you. This tool will help you track your progress and can be used on an ongoing basis to assess the effectiveness of your presence. Building off that assessment, starting in chapter 2, you will develop a customized action plan to build and maintain your Signature Voice. Following the ACE model, you will develop tools and techniques to more consistently, clearly, and confidently exude a presence that is authentic and has impact no matter where you are in your career.

In chapters 3, 4, and 5, we go into detail on each of the components of ACE, a program similar to the conditioning of a master athlete. In chapter 3, you will learn to question and reset your assumptions through mental conditioning. Here we focus on three critical assumptions: what you bring to the table, what perspective you hold, and what matters most to you. Chapter 4 focuses on the communication strategies required for effective leadership presence. You will learn to hone and deepen the critical skills of framing, advocacy, and listening and engagement. In chapter 5, we talk about energy and physical conditioning. In this chapter, you will learn how to manage what your body says, ensure you are visible, and regulate how you resonate.

Once you've completed the ACE conditioning, we'll talk in chapter 6 about how you can continue to enhance and condition your Signature Voice by returning to ACE when new situations cause your presence to slide and infusing your work with purpose and mission. In chapter 7, we explain how managers can use the presence quadrants and ACE model to help direct reports or mentees work on leadership presence.

Throughout this book, you will follow our main characters, John and Terri, who are introduced in chapter 1. They are composite characters—an aggregate of the thousands of clients we have worked with (and learned from) over the years who have successfully found and maintained their Signature Voice. We show where they started out and where they have ended up. In between, you'll meet other characters modeled on clients who have faced some of the common challenges associated with leadership presence. Each of their experiences will show one aspect of the conditioning regimen you'll be developing.

A FINAL THOUGHT

This work is deeply personal to us both. Throughout our careers, both of us have been told that we needed to change, alter, or better develop our presence. While successful, we, too, received the vague performance feedback that left us confused and frustrated. Early in Amy's career, she was told by a manager to go to Harvard Business School because it would "toughen her up." She had been told that she looked too young, that she should try to act older. Some managers had deemed her reflective and conceptual approach as "too soft" or "passive." Muriel represents the opposite side of the spectrum. She had often been told to "tone it down," that she came off too strong and abrasive. Her tendency to be action oriented, pragmatic, and entrepreneurial had been called "too aggressive" and "antagonistic."

We both struggled with this kind of advice and how to deal with the behaviors and attributes that were garnering such criticism. We tried to act like others who had the traits we seemed to lack. We tried on different voices, approaches, and styles. At times, we even tried to ignore the feedback. These attempts failed miserably.

We realized the way to our personal best was not to emulate or ignore others but to embrace who we truly are. It is through that authenticity, and through building capabilities much as an athlete does, that we have been able to impact others in a much stronger way than either of us ever expected. This has been a journey for both of us. We have had to develop the confidence to find our own Signature Voices and in turn have helped thousands of clients do the same.

Welcome to your own journey to Signature Voice.

CHAPTER ONE

FINDING YOUR SIGNATURE VOICE

Meet John

At our first coaching meeting, John explained that he wasn't surprised when Roger, the global managing director, asked to talk over dinner. He knew he was on the short list of those being considered to run the North America practice of the prominent consulting firm they worked for. The current partner in charge of North America was retiring in another eighteen months, and it was no secret that the executive committee was in the throes of selecting his successor. At the restaurant, Roger started by thanking John for a job well done as the managing partner of the Chicago office. The partners had named him to that position over four years ago, and John was steadily leading it to be one of the highest-performing offices in the firm. Roger complimented his performance over the past year, specifically noting how he'd grown the geography's client base and strengthened its recruiting pipeline.

As he listened, John anticipated the "but" he feared was coming. And then Roger said it: "We're optimistic about your future at the firm, but I wanted to give you a heads up that there is a bit of noise surrounding your candidacy that may affect the executive committee's selection." John felt his heart drop. He tried to contain his disappointment.

Roger said that the partnership appreciated his "can-do attitude," his success with the Chicago office, and his reliability as someone who consistently performed well in both firm management and client delivery. The committee was hesitating to name him managing partner for North America for three reasons, he said. One, John did not have enough "weight" in the firm. While he was well liked by those who'd worked with him and was considered very approachable, many of the partners who hadn't worked with him said they couldn't yet judge his capability to lead such a big platform. Two, some partners raised concerns about John's executive presence among the other partners. Specifically, they questioned whether he had what it takes to deal with his peers when negotiating the inevitable conflicts and contentions that would arise in his new role; would he be able to integrate and negotiate between the competing agendas across the North America practice? Three, some of the partners had commented on John's capacity to take on a larger scope of responsibility. He often seemed physically overwhelmed by his current workload.

John knew that he was unproven in many ways, but he was confident that what he brought to the table in leading the Chicago office would bring him the same success in the North America role. He was more shocked by the comment about his ability to deal with the other partners. He believed that his innate abilities of empathy and thoughtfulness made him an excellent leader. He might be less confident in handling peer conflicts, especially if they were politically charged, but he didn't think it showed in his leadership. Principals and junior partners competed to work in the Chicago office and secure him as a mentor. The final blow was the comment about his physical capacity. Yes, John did feel like he was burning the midnight oil more often than he'd like, but he certainly didn't think it showed or that it would become a factor in this promotion. John left his dinner with Roger feeling confused.

Meet Terri

Terri was increasingly defensive as she reviewed her 360 feedback. She was participating in the company's prestigious leadership development program as one of twenty high-potential managers selected each year by the executive management team. The first step of the program was a 360 review, the results of which now sat on the table in front of Terri.

As a vice president in marketing, Terri had always considered herself a rising star, and rightly so. She had worked with Sean, the company's head of marketing, at a previous company. Sean had personally brought Terri on board from their former employer. Because of this relationship, Terri had access to other senior leaders and was well respected by the entire C-suite. Her past feedback had always positively focused on her drive for results, the innovative ideas she brought to the table, and her strong presentation skills.

The feedback from the 360 corroborated these strengths, especially the input from the company's senior leaders. At the same time, it included many comments that pointed to several areas that Terri could work on: listening, building peer relationships, and conflict management. She was especially taken aback by the low ratings from her peers and direct reports. A few of the comments were particularly pointed and negative.

As we talked through the feedback, Terri relayed a recent conversation she had had with Sean. He had told her there was a large, high-visibility role coming up to lead a critical cross-enterprise task force, and he wanted to nominate Terri for the role because of her vision and innovation brilliance. But the job required that Terri collaborate more broadly with peers throughout the enterprise. Sean had said, "I need you to play nicer in the sandbox." When Terri had laughed at this, Sean had explained that he was hearing rumblings. Terri was doing well, of course, but at the most recent talent review, some in the C-suite said they were getting complaints from their direct reports about her often-blunt, slightly arrogant style. Terri had felt annoyed. She looked at us and said,

"This is who I am—a little rough around the edges. But I get the job done better than most people, and everyone knows that."

———————

While seemingly different in career paths and leadership styles, John and Terri had a lot in common. Both had been hugely successful up to this point. John had gone to Ivy League schools. Right out of college, he had worked at a prominent investment bank before heading back to business school. When he had started at the consulting firm, the partnership considered him a star senior associate and he had shot through the ranks to engagement manager and then to principal in record time. He was one of the youngest partners when he reached that level and was quickly tapped to head the Chicago office. Terri had similarly skyrocketed up the career ladder. She was hired at her first company as part of a management rotation program. All the VPs she had worked for wanted her in their division before she landed on marketing. She had spent only four years as a brand manager before being promoted to vice president, one of the fastest moves in the company.

Terri and John also brought a lot of natural talent and strengths to their roles. Throughout his path to office partner, John demonstrated the sound advisory and analytical skills expected of a consultant to solve tough client problems. He was thoughtful and collaborative by nature, and his keen intuition about people allowed him to easily connect with clients and internal team members. Terri, all the way up until she secured the VP title, demonstrated the creativity and execution know-how of a top marketer while leveraging her natural comfort with senior management to push her ideas through.

However, John and Terri had both reached places where their earlier successful approaches were no longer working. Until then, they had played to their natural styles and had been rewarded for it. In Terri's case, that was a strong *voice for self* that conveyed confidence and determination. In John's case, that was a strong *voice for others*—easily connecting with peers, team members, and clients and intuitively understanding and responding to their needs.

For each of them, this approach had worked. But now, as they approached the cusp of the executive level, *what was expected of them had broadened*. This shift exposed vulnerabilities. The less-developed parts of their capability set were becoming more apparent. Roger and the firm's partnership questioned John's suitability for the North America managing partner role. Sean and his fellow C-suite executives raised flags around Terri's ability to align and lead the cross-functional team and consequently doubted her ability to lead at a broader level.

Now, instead of solely relying on their natural styles, they needed to bring together two capabilities: *the ability to demonstrate their value and distinction* and *the ability to connect and align with their stakeholders*. Terri could use more of what John had, and vice versa. When leaders are able to use both capabilities—two voices—and operate "in the zone," they have found their Signature Voice (see figure 1-1).

Neither Terri nor John could rely on the leadership presence that had worked for them in the past. They needed to shift from

FIGURE 1-1

Signature Voice

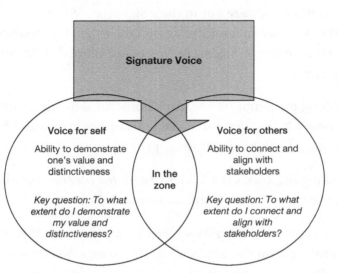

playing to their preferred voice to finding an authentic and connected voice that was adaptable to evolving circumstances. But
the question was: how?

A NEW WAY OF DIAGNOSING PRESENCE

It bears repeating: Terri and John were both *very* successful. They
were not remedial cases, and their careers were not at risk. But
Roger and Sean, and the others who had given them feedback,
were pointing out the cracks: the situations and circumstances
in which they didn't display the leadership presence needed to
meet expectations. So if Terri and John were not in their Signature
Voice, where exactly were they?

Perhaps you've found yourself in a similar position: despite tremendous success in your current role, there are times when the
situation or circumstances change, and what it means to be most
effective changes too. When this happens, how can you find a way
to consistently demonstrate leadership presence? To help individuals unpack this question, we've developed a diagnostic tool called
the *presence quadrants.* We have helped thousands of people use
this tool to diagnose their presence and better understand what
happens when they are not in their Signature Voice.

In the presence quadrants, we've taken the two capabilities of
presence inherent in Signature Voice and plotted them against a
2×2 matrix:

- Along the y-axis, is a leader's *voice for self*—the ability to
  convey his or her (and usually his or her team's and functions') distinction and value proposition.

- Along the x-axis is a leader's *voice for others*—the ability to
  connect with, align, and impact stakeholders.

Leaders move up the y-axis when their voice for self is stronger.
They move out on the x-axis when they strengthen their voice for
others. When they are able to use these two voices in an integrated

FIGURE 1-2

Presence quadrants

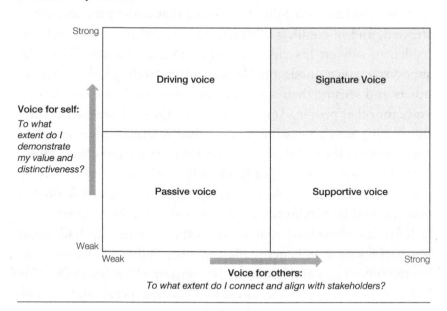

way, they achieve a Signature Voice. The goal is to consistently hit that upper right-hand quadrant in any situation or with any audience, so that you are drawing on both voices as needed. A good tennis player will have a stronger forehand or a stronger backhand and will favor that strength. An exceptional tennis player will have a strong forehand and a strong backhand *and* will masterfully rely on the one that is going to help her win each point, and use them in concert to win the match. Similarly, when you are in Signature Voice, you have a strong voice for self and voice for others and know which to use, when.

But the reality is, when your role becomes bigger, the decisions you need to influence become more complex, or you're under more and more stress, it's natural to seek out your comfort zone and lean more heavily on one axis than the other, like a tennis player whose preferred swing is her backhand. This is when your presence slides to one of the other quadrants. In these situations, natural tendencies, preferences, and styles take over. And when that happens, as it did with John and Terri, people begin to question their leadership potential.

As we worked with John, he realized that under pressure, when stressed, and in conflicts with partners he did not know well, he tended to subvert his voice for self, and his presence slid to the supportive voice quadrant. He was instinctively good at reading others and sensing their agendas and needs. He had a very strong voice for other people. At moments when the staff needed rallying, this quality was an enormous asset and it largely contributed to his success as the managing partner for the Chicago office. However, this same tendency got in his way as a member of the larger partnership group, a role that required he represent his office's interests and be perceived as a peer to other top firm leaders.

John acknowledged that as the office partner he had spent much of his time and energy playing a heads-down role, supporting the office team and handling the constant client fire drills. This last year especially, his workload had become increasingly unsustainable as he was stretched in all directions trying to meet client needs, the new business development needs of the office, and the needs of his team. A natural tendency to put other's needs before his own, especially when on autopilot, was getting in the way. He was exhausted and burned-out by the stress and the realization that he could no longer do it all as he could when he had less responsibility.

To develop the presence required to take on the larger role, John needed to increase his voice for self and shift out of the lower right-hand quadrant—supportive voice. This required understanding how he was currently perceived and developing an aspiration for how others would view him. He needed to move from being seen as great at execution and supporting the agenda of the office, team, and clients to being known as someone who provides strategic direction and firm leadership to his fellow partners.

As we worked with Terri, we were able to show her on the presence quadrants that with Sean and other senior leaders, she was consistently in the upper right-hand quadrant: Signature Voice.

But with her direct reports and peers, with whom she tended to have less patience: her presence slid to the driving voice quadrant, and she was perceived as a bull in a china shop. She had a strong voice for self but had more difficulty connecting with her peers or direct reports. With her peers, she was more likely to speak her mind and "call it as she saw it." Most of her colleagues acknowledged that she was often right, but her delivery left people feeling trodden upon or intimidated. Terri admitted that when she was in a discussion she felt wasn't relevant or was going nowhere, she became more terse, abrupt, and impatient. What she failed to see was how negatively that impacted others and how it created a perception that she was difficult to work with.

Senior management happily overlooked the noise when Terri was in more functional roles. But now that they were considering her for a more senior role that required cross-functional oversight and collaboration, they questioned whether she could see beyond herself or her team and drive the alignment and coordination necessary for success at the executive level. Terri's work was to increase her voice for others and shift away from driving voice toward Signature Voice. She needed to leave behind the perception that she had a single line of vision and drove for results without aligning or bringing along others. Instead, she needed to evolve into a visionary who is able to mobilize others.

Leaders like Terri and John (and pretty much everyone!) are engaged in a constant effort to integrate two human instincts: the desire to connect and relate to others and the desire to assert an independent self. As they move into more complex, more demanding roles, they are challenged by the new responsibilities and expectations. And when they're faced with that stress or are simply tired and overworked, they retreat to their comfort zone and lean too heavily in one direction or another.

The challenge all individuals face is to *use both voices strategically and adaptively*: to speak for yourself, your team, and your function and to know when to do the same for others, their teams, and their functions. As you move along the leadership pipeline and

FIGURE 1-3

Adapting your voice to fit your role

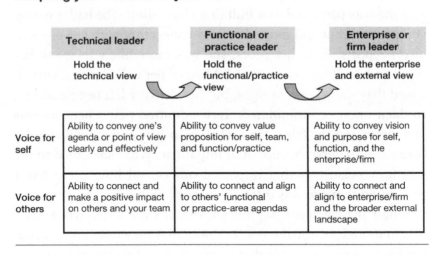

	Technical leader Hold the technical view	Functional or practice leader Hold the functional/practice view	Enterprise or firm leader Hold the enterprise and external view
Voice for self	Ability to convey one's agenda or point of view clearly and effectively	Ability to convey value proposition for self, team, and function/practice	Ability to convey vision and purpose for self, function, and the enterprise/firm
Voice for others	Ability to connect and make a positive impact on others and your team	Ability to connect and align to others' functional or practice-area agendas	Ability to connect and align to enterprise/firm and the broader external landscape

the demands of new roles increase, you must adapt your voice for self and voice for others, expanding your abilities to demonstrate your value and to connect and align with others (see figure 1-3).

ASSESSING WHERE YOUR PRESENCE SLIDES

Determining where your presence slides is not always easy. John and Terri spent lots of time trying to understand what happened when they were not at their personal best or felt particularly challenged or frustrated. They thought hard about what their new roles required of their voice for self and voice for others. Here is what each voice looks, sounds, and feels like. As you read through these descriptions, pay attention to what resonates and think about which quadrant you are most often susceptible to.

Supportive Voice Quadrant

THIS IS WHAT IT LOOKS LIKE TO OTHERS. People see you as collaborative and approachable. Colleagues often seek your advice, confident that you will be able to see their perspective in the situation without judgment. (And because of this more accommodating tendency, a lot of people automatically—and mistakenly—ascribe this quadrant to women; see "A Word on Signature Voice for Women" on this and other issues.) You take time making decisions because you believe that considering multiple perspectives ultimately leads to a better solution. However, to some of your colleagues, you seem slow to make tough decisions, especially when they negatively affect others, as in the case of personnel or reorganization decisions. While you are valued for appreciating multiple perspectives, it's sometimes unclear to others your own stake in the matter.

THIS IS WHAT IT SOUNDS LIKE. People who slide to this quadrant often say or think things like:

> "A lot of people are counting on us; we can't let them down."

> "They aren't going to like our viewpoint on this. I'm worried about damaging our relationship."

> "The executive team is breathing down our necks and they want it done a certain way. We'll need to change tack again."

> "I need more information before making the final call."

THIS IS WHAT IT FEELS LIKE TO YOU. You are rarely the first to speak or offer an opinion in a meeting, as you'd prefer to listen and observe first. You are often offended by colleagues who use up time trying to be heard rather than offer anything substantive. You spend a sizeable amount of your time and energy considering the various players and people involved in a situation and trying to anticipate others' responses. You use that information and try to avoid having a difficult conversation or negotiation. You often feel stretched and blame others for creating unrealistic priorities and deadlines for you and your team. Because you are naturally service oriented, you also feel the tension of wanting to uphold your commitments to others, often at the expense of your or your team's time and your own health. You are concerned about what others think and how you can communicate in a way that meets their needs, and you use body language that some interpret as a lack of self-confidence.

A WORD ON SIGNATURE VOICE FOR WOMEN

We are often asked if we see more women slide to one of the quadrants more than others. Do women tend to have a stronger supportive voice, since they are stereotypically more nurturing and focused on others? We understand why people ask the question. But among the thousands of women we've worked with, we don't see such a trend. What we have observed is that our female clients have a stronger voice for self as often as they have a stronger voice for others. The same is true for men: there are just as many who slide to supportive voice as driving voice.

However, we *do* see a difference in how women are treated. Women tend to be overly penalized when they slide to either voice, compared with their male counterparts. Managers judge them more harshly. This observation is substantiated by research about women and presence. For example, a 2007 study by Catalyst described a "double bind" in which women executives feel as though they are caught in the quintessential "damned if you do, damned if you don't" quandary as it relates to their presence.[1] The research shows that women are perceived in extreme ranges of either being too soft or too tough, too supportive or too driving. They are viewed as competent or likable, but rarely both. Women need to be aware of this systemic bias and address it by doing what's in their control: finding a consistent, confident leadership presence. Many of our female clients have done just this. While it doesn't change the prejudice against them, it does improve other's perceptions and their own performance.

The supportive voice quadrant is where John's presence slid. As he rose through the firm, he took on more and more responsibility. He enjoyed knowing he was needed and was resistant to letting anything fall to someone else's shoulders. Eventually, he staggered under the weight of an overwhelming workload. While people across the firm were drawn to his approachability, his peers sometimes grew frustrated by his lack of clear direction. After hearing the feedback from Roger, he too wondered whether he had what it takes to run North America.

Driving Voice Quadrant

THIS IS WHAT IT LOOKS LIKE TO OTHERS. Others see you as driven and focused. They view you as successful in advocating your own, your team's, or your function's agenda, but they feel you sometimes fail to acknowledge or completely disregard others' agendas. You impress others with your line of vision and ability to drive results, particularly as you've risen through the ranks of your organization. But along the way, you may have rubbed others the wrong way. Those around you describe your style as "direct," "judgmental," "demanding," or "confident." To some, that confidence may even be perceived as arrogance. You appear to think mostly about yourself. Your mind-set, the way you communicate, and the energy you give off are about you, your team, and your agenda.

THIS IS WHAT IT SOUNDS LIKE. People who slide to this quadrant often say or think things like:

> "What does my team stand to gain or lose from this?"

> "Why can't we make the decision and move on?"

> "This is the right thing to do, even if people don't realize it yet."

> "Why is everyone being so sensitive?"

THIS IS WHAT IT FEELS LIKE TO YOU. You often feel impatient with others. In meetings, you wish they would move faster, speak in bullet points, grasp ideas quickly, and move on when a decision is made. Building consensus and aligning others feels painful. You work best when you have direct authority over a team or are in the presence of senior management. You see a clear line from point A to point B, and if it were left up to you alone, you know you would get the job done. You have little tolerance for incompetence, and when things go wrong, you tend to blame others or the environment. Because you thrive on a fast pace and a feeling of accomplishment, you are surprised that other people don't feel a same sense of urgency.

The driving voice quadrant is where Terri's presence slid, especially in situations with her peers and direct reports. Naturally assertive, she loved driving to results. When she wanted to move things forward, she relied on her persuasiveness and decisiveness. Some of her direct reports and peers thought of her as gruff and short-tempered. More often than not, they felt she was crossing the thin line between confident and arrogant. Although she had achieved a great deal of success, Terri was receiving feedback that this approach, while perhaps permissible for her current role, could hamper her next step up the ladder.

Terri is in good company. Many executives who have worked their way to the top of organizations slide into the driving voice quadrant. Consider Tony Hayward, the CEO of BP at the time of the 2010 *Deepwater Horizon* oil spill. While the world was reeling from the potentially disastrous effects of the largest oil spill in history, Hayward was quoted in the *New York Times* as asking his executive team, "What the hell did we do to deserve this?" A few months later he was quoted as saying, "I want my life back." Hayward was lambasted for his insensitivity, his refusal to accept responsibility, and his downright selfishness. BP's board eventually forced him to leave his role. What Hayward failed to articulate, and perhaps to understand, was the devastating impact his company's actions had on others.

Passive Voice Quadrant

We haven't yet talked much about the lower left-hand quadrant: the passive voice. This quadrant is more complex than the others, and yet we see just as many individuals slide here. Almost everyone has moments when neither a voice for self or voice for others is strong and clear. This results in a wide range of perceptions: people may describe others who end up here as passive, a wallflower, passive-aggressive, defensive, shut down, or disengaged. For every person, this particular quadrant manifests itself differently. Take Toyota Motor Corporation president Akio Toyoda. During the 2010 recall of millions of Toyota vehicles for what was thought to be a malfunction, Toyoda was heavily criticized for his handling of the crisis and, in particular, how he handled himself as a leader. The *Wall Street Journal* described it this way: "The crisis has shone a harsh light on Mr. Toyoda's management style, and on the company's management structure as well. Mr. Toyoda's actions since the safety crisis unfurled—including flying to Davos, Switzerland, just as the U.S. recalls were announced, vacillating last week on whether he would attend the congressional hearings in Washington and generally staying behind the scenes—have led onlookers to question whether he is a decisive, confident leader."[2] This is a clear example of a leader who, under the pressure of an extreme crisis, did not maintain his presence. Instead, Mr. Toyoda slid to the passive voice, with serious consequences for his company and himself, in the form of billion-dollar losses.[3] His story is a good reminder that even at the highest leadership levels, one's presence can slide.

Unfortunately, staying in this quadrant too long can severely impair an individual's career. People end up here by doing a "double slide": their presence first slides to supportive or driving voice and then, when they do nothing about it, their presence slides again, this time into passive voice. Table 1-1 explains how this happens and what it looks like.

Paul is a perfect example of the double slide from driving voice. He is a senior statistician at the health research center he's worked at for over fifteen years. He is seen as an expert in his organization and his field. Because of this expertise, he is confident about his opinion and often says exactly what he thinks in meetings with his direct reports and his boss, at times coming off as too directive or gruff.

He is technically strong, precise, and logical and can easily focus on the minute details of his programs for weeks at a time. Paul's boss thinks he is brilliant, but is not sure Paul can ever be a leader at the research center. He is concerned about Paul's presence, particularly when he is in meetings with large groups or senior executives, where everyone is expected to share ideas and collaborate. His boss is confused because Paul easily speaks up and articulates his viewpoint in the smaller meetings with his team, but in larger forums, he comes off as hard to read or even passively flying under the radar. Those outside of his immediate sphere get frustrated with him when he agrees to one thing in those meetings but then does something different afterward.

When we work with the Pauls of the world, we always start by asking, "Do you really want to become a more senior leader?" because often they are happy with where they are: in technical or individual contributor roles. But if they aspire to greater levels of people management or leadership, they find themselves in an uncomfortable place. They feel as though, despite their well-intentioned efforts, their hard work is not being valued.

While it's important to know that this double slide happens, this book focuses on the initial slide to driving voice or supportive voice. If your presence does slide to passive voice, follow a simple rule of thumb. Instead of trying to work on both voices at the same time, choose one to focus on first. If your presence tends to slide to driving voice and has subsequently slid to passive voice, then work on your voice for others first and then your voice for self. Likewise, if your presence tends to slide to supportive voice

TABLE 1-1

Passive voice

If your presence first slides to . . .	This is what it feels like when your presence slides to passive voice	This is what it looks like to others	People say things like . . .
Driving voice	• You hit a point of frustration in a given situation, where your assertive approach isn't working. • You feel like you're not getting through, despite sincere attempts. • You check out and feel angry. • When people try to ask you what is going on, you feel even more annoyed.	• You appear disengaged, checked out. • It looks like you've retreated into a corner. • Others think of you as hard to read or unpredictable.	• "They don't get it at all." • "This is a stupid waste of my time." • "Why bother?"
Supportive voice	• You sense a conflict between what others want and what you want. • To buy yourself time to assess the situation or figure out how to move forward, you retreat. • You fear disappointing others, so you don't respond to e-mails or requests for time.	• People are confused by your actions and wonder why you seem to have disappeared when you are normally so present. • They seek you out to resolve the situation but feel like you simply aren't there. • They think of you as flying under the radar.	• "Why are they pressuring me to make a decision?" • "Why can't they just leave me alone?"

and you find yourself in passive voice, work on your voice for self and then your voice for others. This will allow you to find your way back to Signature Voice.

MAKE YOUR OWN DIAGNOSIS

The starting point to achieving Signature Voice is to understand where and why your presence slides. Which of the axes—voice for self or voice for others—comes naturally to you? Which one takes more effort? In what situations do you reactively move out of Signature Voice and into one of the other quadrants? The drill below will help you make your own diagnosis. Knowing which quadrant you slide to *most often* is key. This is your baseline—and from there, you can start working towards the goal of consistent Signature Voice.

You may be wondering, "Aren't there times when my presence should be in driving voice or in supportive voice? Aren't there situations where focusing on 'I' or 'you' instead of 'we' is effective?" This is a question we get asked a lot, and we emphatically say *yes*, there are situations or circumstances when you should strategically use one or the other voice more. But the key is to do it *consciously*—rather than on autopilot—and to remain in that upper right-hand quadrant while leaning on the voice that will be most effective for the situation or audience at hand. For example, when Terri is presenting to the C-Suite, she may strategically lean more heavily on her voice for others in the hope of meeting the high demands of her superiors while still being mindful of her own agenda. Similarly, when John is working with the CEO of one of the client accounts he leads, he can be appropriately assertive, drawing on his voice for self while keeping track of the CEO's reaction and perspective.

You should never fully abandon one voice for the other. You can adamantly disagree with a colleague and express your voice for self without ever losing sight of the other person by maintaining an appropriate level of engagement and respect (voice for others). A senior managing partner at a private equity firm once told us, "It's all about having confidence whereby one can feel strongly about a point of view and not lose track of the other."

This integration is critical. Those who have mastered Signature Voice can adeptly oscillate from voice for self to voice for others and back, conveying a presence that is approachable and consistent. Signature Voice is ultimately about discovering what's possible when you are capable of embracing and using both voices.

DRILL

Find Your Slide

Figure 1-4 is an exercise we use with our clients to understand their own slides to the various quadrants:

1. List six people who you interact with regularly. Choose two direct reports, two peers, and two people who are senior to you. If relevant, select at least one person outside the organization such as a client or strategic partner. Think about how you interact with each person.

2. Remember a time when you were not at your personal best: which quadrant did you move to? Which voice did you lose sight of?

3. Plot where you fall on the presence quadrants in your interactions with each stakeholder.

What Patterns Emerge?

Now look at your list. Ask yourself: "What patterns can I identify? Do you consistently slide to one voice or another? Do you slide to one voice with people above you and another with your peers?

Here are some of the patterns leaders have identified in our coaching and training programs after working through this exercise:

(continued)

FIGURE 1-4

Understand your slides to the various quadrants

List six stakeholders (internal or external; two senior, two peers, two direct reports) with whom you have one-to-one interactions. Make an assessment of the quadrant you move toward with each of these stakeholders when you are *not* at your personal best.

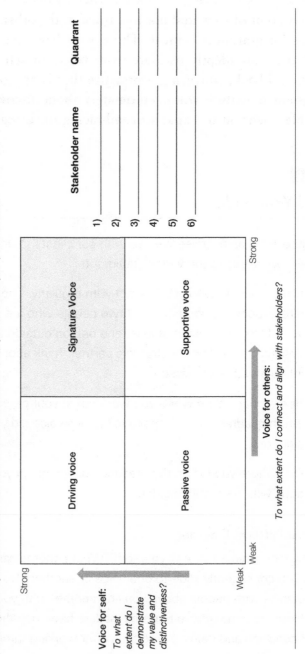

Stakeholder name   **Quadrant**

1) _____   _____

2) _____   _____

3) _____   _____

4) _____   _____

5) _____   _____

6) _____   _____

Strong

Driving voice   Signature Voice

Voice for self:
*To what
extent do I
demonstrate
my value and
distinctiveness?*

Passive voice   Supportive voice

Weak

Weak   Strong

Voice for others:
To what extent do I connect and align with stakeholders?

"I realized I default to driving voice when there is a lot on my plate. My drive for results is such a strength, but sometimes it goes on overdrive and I unintentionally exclude others or fail to bring them along as I need to in this role."

"Depending on the situation or stakeholder, my exercise showed that I move to all the quadrants. I default to driving voice with my direct report team but I can also move to supportive, or even passive, voice with the executive leadership team. The 360-degree feedback flagged that the executive leadership team doesn't have enough visibility into what I do."

There are no right or wrong answers here. The important thing is to get out of autopilot and begin to see how you operate and show up with others.

WHAT TO REMEMBER

- Leaders need to bring together two capabilities:

  - *Voice for self:* The ability to demonstrate your value and distinction

  - *Voice for others:* The ability to connect and align with your stakeholders

- When leaders are able to use both capabilities—two voices—and operate "in the zone," they have found their Signature Voice.

- The challenge all individuals face is to *adaptively use both voices*: to speak for yourself, your team, and your function and to know when to do the same for others, their teams, and their functions. As you move along the leadership pipeline and the demands on you increase, you must adapt your voice for self and voice for others, expanding your abilities to demonstrate your value and to connect and align with others.

- When a leader's voice for self is stronger, her presence slides out of Signature Voice to driving voice. When a leader's voice for others is stronger, his presence slides out of Signature Voice to supportive voice.

- There are situations or circumstances when you should strategically use voice for self more than your voice others and vice versa. But you should never fully abandon one voice for the other. It's about strengthening both so you can use them agilely.

CHAPTER TWO

HOW DO I GET TO
SIGNATURE VOICE?

When John realized the partners perceived him as an effective office partner but not necessarily as global leadership team material, it was an emotional moment. First, he was frustrated to find out that all his hard work, while good enough to lead the Chicago office, did not qualify him for the North America managing partner position. He wondered if he had been wasting his time? Second, he questioned his ability to take his leadership presence to the next level. Could he change the perception the partners had of him? Would he be able to adapt his presence to be more effective with his team and with a broader set of partners? Could he increase his voice for self and overcome the slide to supportive voice? There was no question in John's mind that he wanted to build the next level of his Signature Voice. But his angst was about how to get there. In our initial meeting with him, he said, "I now understand the feedback. But I have no idea how to *address* it."

Likewise, Terri was confounded about how to address what she heard from her stakeholders. Beyond being annoyed, she doubted that changing her presence was going to have any effect. She wondered out loud whether altering her presence would make her less effective and ultimately hurt the organization. But she wanted to lead the cross-functional task force and move on to greater leadership roles. She didn't like that her slide to driving voice prevented her from her goals. She too asked us how to tackle her dilemma.

Realizing that your presence is not getting you the results you want can be surprising and demoralizing. In fact, when leaders realize where on the presence quadrants they have slid to, they question:

- If I *know* it's not useful to be in that quadrant, why do I keep sliding there?

- Can I really change, or is this just who I am?

- How will I ever make it to the next level with this kind of pattern?

- What's standing in the way of my being more assertive or more collaborative or more sensitive to others?

MOVING TO HOW: FROM FEEDBACK TO SIGNATURE VOICE

The answer to "How?" can be found in the clues that emerge from the feedback we got from Terri and John's colleagues. We spoke with twelve of John's stakeholders, including eight partners and four team members. This is what we heard:

- John takes a tactical view of the business when he should be stepping back and seeing the big picture. He's playing a narrow game, which he's good at, but he needs to be playing a different game altogether: a more expansive, global one.

- It's unclear where John wants to take his career. He needs to find the intersection between what he's passionate about and where the firm his headed. Once he's done that, he needs to articulate it to the rest of us with a clear plan of action.

- John tries to get things done incrementally, getting approval along the way. He could be stronger and clearer in his communications. I'd like to hear him say: "This is where we're going. This is how we're going to get there. And this is the support we need."

- John can't allow himself to get ruffled by conflict or firm politics. He needs to be consistent, put a stake in the ground, and not back down. This is especially critical when he's in the room with the other North American partners. He could prove his mettle as a leader by finding ways to navigate the politics and integrate various points of view.

- John seems overwhelmed. He'll agree to take something on, no matter how busy he is. He needs to prioritize and delegate. It doesn't even seem like he uses his executive assistant to handle scheduling and help with time management.

- John looks like he's drained all the time. Even if he's frazzled, he should work on giving the impression that he isn't. His being spread too thin has a negative impact on him physically. He looks burned-out and as though he's not taking care of himself. He should prioritize his health and appearance.

Here's what we heard when we spoke with Terri's stakeholders:

- Every sentence starts with "I," which makes you think that all she cares about is herself. I know she cares about other things, but it doesn't always show.

- Terri gives the impression she's always advocating for her team and their agenda: her lens is, "What's in it for marketing?"

- Terri has little patience for small talk. She wants to cut right to the chase.

- She can drive a point home like no one else I know. She is direct and concise. It works for me, but I know that others wish she would take the time to explain.

- She is always the last one to come into a meeting, and she looks like she's in a rush. Her body language tells everyone, "Let's get this over with as soon as possible." It makes us feel pressured.

- I've caught her looking at her watch multiple times during conversations. It's a bad message to send to the team.

While these may seem like laundry lists of unconnected issues, a closer look at the feedback reveals that the perceptions John and Terri's subordinates, peers, and superiors raise fall into three categories:

- What they are thinking

- What they are saying

- How they express themselves physically

Go back and look at the feedback again. The first two bullet points for each of them match Terri and John's mind-set and assumptions—what they are thinking. The next few comments are about their communication strategies—what they are saying. The last few are about the physical energy they give off. *Leadership presence is the aggregate of these three things: what you believe, how you communicate, and the energy you express to others.*

Over the years, to help clients remember these drivers of presence, we created the ACE model, an acronym for *assumptions, communication strategies,* and *energy.* Together they are a system, and if any part of this system is out of whack, it will affect the others and cause a slide to one of the other three presence quadrants. When building your Signature Voice, *you need to focus on the entire system, not just one aspect.*

Terri may have taken the feedback she received and understood it to be about how she communicated with her peers. She may have made a concerted effort to demonstrate concern and interest in their opinions by asking questions and paraphrasing back what she heard. But if she assumed that she knew the right answer regardless of what they said, her effort to convey concern would have failed. Or if she continued to sit through meetings signaling negative energy—arms crossed, constantly checking her watch— her peers would see right through her. Instead, Terri needed to think about all three levers and condition herself in each area.

Figure 2-1 shows how your assumptions, communication strategies, and energy can manifest themselves in each quadrant. Using your diagnostic from chapter 1, look at the quadrant that you most often slide to. Then look at the Signature Voice quadrant. By demonstrating the attributes in that quadrant, you enhance your leadership presence.

IN THE SPOTLIGHT: MAYOR FENTY AND THE IMPACT OF ACE

It's not only corporate leaders like John and Terri whose presence slides when their roles get larger. Adrian Fenty, the mayor of Washington, DC, from 2007 to 2011, is a prime example. When he ran for mayor, as a councilman from the District of Columbia's Ward 4, pundits doubted he could win. He was up against the council chair who had been in DC politics for twenty-five years and had been endorsed by the retiring mayor, Anthony Williams.[1] But Fenty, who was only thirty-five when he started his campaign, used an aggressive—and uncommon—grassroots strategy, in which he vowed to knock on every door in the city. It worked: not only did he defeat his old establishment opponent but he was also the first candidate in history to win each of DC's 142 precincts.[2]

As a councilman, Fenty was well known for his tenacity, ability to get results and easy connection with people from all walks of life. He had a reputation for quickly responding to constituent

FIGURE 2-1

How assumptions, communication strategies, and energy manifest in each quadrant

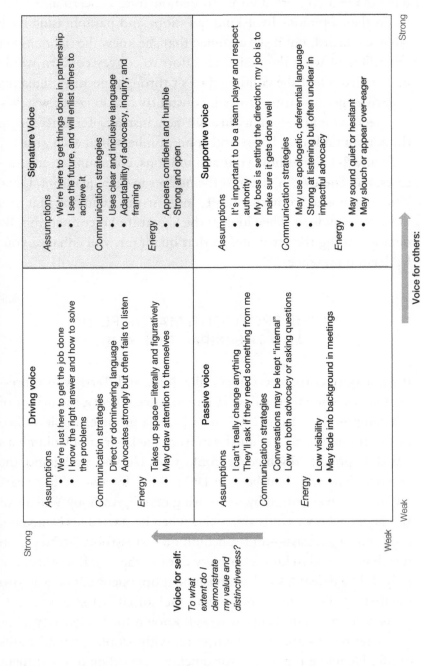

Driving voice

Assumptions
- We're just here to get the job done
- I know the right answer and how to solve the problems

Communication strategies
- Direct or domineering language
- Advocates strongly but often fails to listen

Energy
- Takes up space—literally and figuratively
- May draw attention to themselves

Signature Voice

Assumptions
- We're here to get things done in partnership
- I see the future, and will enlist others to achieve it

Communication strategies
- Uses clear and inclusive language
- Adaptability of advocacy, inquiry, and framing

Energy
- Appears confident and humble
- Strong and open

Passive voice

Assumptions
- I can't really change anything
- They'll ask if they need something from me

Communication strategies
- Conversations may be kept "internal"
- Low on both advocacy or asking questions

Energy
- Low visibility
- May fade into background in meetings

Supportive voice

Assumptions
- It's important to be a team player and respect authority
- My boss is setting the direction; my job is to make sure it gets done well

Communication strategies
- May use apologetic, deferential language
- Strong at listening but often unclear in impactful advocacy

Energy
- May sound quiet or hesitant
- May slouch or appear over-eager

Strong

Weak

Weak

Strong

Voice for others:
To what extent do I connect and align with stakeholders?

Voice for self:
To what extent do I demonstrate my value and distinctiveness?

complaints and going head-to-head with the local agencies to re-solve issues and fight against government inefficiency. His ward benefited from this approach: garbage was quickly picked up, crime decreased, new businesses opened their doors. His constitu-ents lauded him for both his hard-charging style and his accessi-bility. They told stories of sending e-mails to his office, sometimes about the smallest of concerns, and receiving a reply within min-utes from Fenty himself promising to take care of the issue.[3] As a councilman, Fenty conveyed a presence that was clear about what he brought to his ward and was connected to the people who ben-efited from his work. He had a Signature Voice and was clearly in the upper right-hand quadrant.

Four years after he was elected, things were very different for Mayor Fenty. During his doomed reelection campaign, the press no longer featured him as someone adored by his constituents. In fact, the *Washington City Paper* ran an article with the headline: "Is Adrian Fenty a Jerk?"[4] The city's voters had turned against him, despite the clear advances he accomplished. How had Fenty gone from a revered councilman with a strong presence to an un-electable mayor who was lambasted by many of those who once supported him? Fenty slid from the sweet spot of Signature Voice to driving voice *because he did not effectively adapt his presence to meet the demands of his new role.*

We can use the ACE model to understand how this slide oc-curred:

- Fenty had made a *false assumption*—that what had made him a great councilman would work for him as mayor. He took the same aggressive approach that had worked in his ward—making changes swiftly, responding to every con-stituent need, pushing for results—but it didn't translate into his new role.

- Because of this assumption, he was overly direct and dismissive of others, leading to a *communication gap*. He wasn't able to be in close contact with his constituents the way he had previously been. He tended to make decisions, such as the hiring of controversial school chancellor Michelle Rhee, without gaining buy-in from the necessary stakeholders. He gained a reputation as someone who was unable or unwilling to listen. At community meetings, people perceived him as aloof and insensitive to the issues they raised.[5] This was a stark contrast to the responsive councilman who returned e-mails in a matter of minutes.

- People also criticized Fenty for his *physical presence* and the energy he gave off. At a summer funeral for a train operator killed in one of the city metro's deadliest crashes, he showed up an hour late and wore a light-colored summer suit, which was interpreted as inappropriate.[6]

As you can see, Fenty's slide was not the function of one incident or one behavior; it was the result of a concert of things: first, the false assumptions about his role and what he brought to the table; second, ineffective communication and a failure to listen to constituents and other stakeholders; and third, inability to convey through his physical presence and energy that he was connected with those around him.

HOW ACE WORKS

The ACE model—the *how* of Signature Voice—not only provides clues to what is weakening your presence but it can also give you an actionable way forward. By working through each component of ACE, you gain a clear prescription for how to build Signature Voice. The model serves leaders in the following ways.

ACE Helps Leaders Interpret Feedback and Take Action

Terri and John's stories have a different ending from Fenty's in large part because they were able to hear and understand their feedback and do something about it using the ACE model. Fenty refused to heed the advice of those around him, even his closest advisers. Many tried to convince him to make changes and adapt his leadership style, but he stiff-armed them and stuck to what he thought would work.[7] Fenty was so determined that he was on the right course—so firmly in driving voice—that he even refused to use pollsters during much of his reelection campaign.[8] The unwillingness to listen to and accept feedback about how others perceive you is one of the biggest obstacles to building leadership presence.

Had Fenty been able to hear what his critics were saying and taken action on that feedback, would he have been reelected in 2010 and led the city for a second term? We can't say for sure, of course. But we do know that openness to learning how others perceive how you think, speak, and show up is a prerequisite to building a Signature Voice.

ACE Helps Leaders Marry Intent with Impact

We see client after client, when they look at the feedback from their stakeholders, despair over what to do next, how to interpret what's been said about their presence. It's important to realize that it's not for lack of trying that they haven't honed their presence.

John worked hard to be collaborative and engage others in to solutions. Yet that is not what others perceived. The firm's partners and even some of his own team members questioned whether he had the backbone to make the tough decisions necessary at the next level. Similarly, Terri felt she was doing her best for the organization by driving for results and pushing those around her to achieve. But not everyone appreciated her style, and many felt she acted more like an inconsiderate bully than an effective leader. Terri's quest to rise to the top of the organization was hindered by this perception that she wasn't a team player.

Many of our clients reach a point when the presence they convey fails to get them the desired results. It is incredibly frustrating for leaders when their impact doesn't line up with their intention.

Try as they might, the result is something different, and usually something less, than what they want.

We often tell our coaching clients that the more senior you become, the more perception matters. You are increasingly under a microscope. Your team members, peers, and superiors interpret your every thought, word, and gesture with greater nuance. And these interpretations drive how they respond to you. Therefore, it's important to *align your intention with your impact*. Ask yourself: What is Signature Voice for me in this situation, with this audience, and in this role? What would my personal best be? Once you are clear on your intention, then condition and prepare your assumptions, communication strategies, and energy to be congruent with the impact you want to have and the results you want to achieve.

Most executives run into trouble when their presence is not congruent with their intentions or where they are in the leadership pipeline. When this happens, the cracks begin to show. ACE gives leaders a way to realign the assumptions, communications strategies, and energy they need for where they are in the pipeline. Figure 2-2 articulates the expectations of a leader as she moves from managing herself, to managing others, and eventually to managing the enterprise, using the ACE model as a lens.

ACE Honors Your Strengths

ACE conditioning helps leaders get to their personal best more often and more consistently. In fact, inherent to Signature Voice is the need to maintain the voice you are naturally skilled at while increasing your facility with the other. Terri knew how to put a stake in the ground—she never hesitated to nail home a point, and her team benefited from this strength. John trusted his intuitive read on other people and effortlessly understood their agendas. Neither lost sight of those strengths as they worked on the other aspects of ACE to increase their competence with voice for self or voice for others.

FIGURE 2-2

Expectations of a leader at increasing levels of responsibility

	Manage self	Manage teams and groups/clients		Manage enterprise/firm
Assumptions	View of team and unit	Transition to broader view	Can see multiple perspectives to support overall business objectives	Has full view of the enterprise/firm, understanding value of each function; broad frame of reference, including industry and world at large
Communication strategies	Sharing technical expertise and perspective	Managing and negotiating boundaries with other groups	Communicating through multiple layers; skilled interpreter and seeker of information	Inspiring and mobilizing others across the enterprise/firm
Energy	Nonverbal congruency; limited and local sphere of influence	Self-management of tone and mood; increased sphere of influence	Setting tone and mood of function; considerable visibility and sphere	Highly visible; wide ripple effect in organization with functional heads, senior management, and external stakeholders

Note: Adapted from Ram Charan, Stephen Drotter, and James Noel, *The Leadership Pipeline* (San Francisco: Jossey-Bass, 2000).

By embracing the less preferred axis, John and Terri took their success to a whole new level. Now, Terri still feels great when she drives a point home, but she makes that point in a way that resonates with her audience and forges a connection with others, rather than intimidating them with her directness. Similarly, John loves when he is able to intuit someone's unspoken issue, but he goes beyond that understanding to address it directly, rather than subverting his own viewpoint to appease or control the individual's reaction.

Think about your strengths: What is it that you bring to the table? How do you feel when you're in this zone? Can you think of times when you could feel others in the room look at each other and think, "We can always trust that person to do *that* thing"? Don't lose sight of that. Use ACE conditioning to bring forth more of your best self.

ACE CONDITIONING—AN INTEGRATED SYSTEM

While we present each component of the ACE model as three separate levers, they are inextricably linked. For example, if you have the mind-set, "I'm not a peer to this executive; I should be deferential to authority," this is going to come through in what you say and how you appear. If you overuse the phrase "I'm sorry," it will reinforce your assumption that you are not a peer and need permission and cause you to hunch more. Likewise, if you are not at your physical best—perhaps you are tired or stressed out—you are more likely to hunch, reinforcing your belief that you need to be deferential and this leads to further requests for permission. Table 2-1 illustrates two examples of how the ACE levers work in concert.

Everyone has a baseline ACE—the place they are starting from when they begin to condition themselves for Signature Voice. We find that what works best is to do an initial assessment and then create a vision of where you want to be. Tables 2-2 and 2-3, respectively, show the roadmaps we created for John and Terri, plotting their baseline against where they wanted to be in terms of ACE. Their ACE baseline was based on the feedback from stakeholders. We then identified the capabilities they needed to develop to achieve Signature Voice in the roles they aspired to. By organizing the feedback and actions in this way, we were able to provide each of them with a clear path forward.

TABLE 2-1

How ACE levers work in concert

Leadership situation	Assumptions	Communication	Energy	Quadrant your presence ends up in	Business impact
	What you think and feel in the situation	*What you end up saying*	*How you end up showing up*		
You are leading a major change initiative in your organization.	"The success of our business is contingent on this change. Whether we like it or not, we have to see it through."	You end up not listening to the concerns and questions voiced by others in the organization. You do not acknowledge how challenging the change may be for others.	You come off as cold and out of touch with key stakeholders.	Driving voice	Many in the organization become demoralized. They comply with the change but are not committed to it over the long term.
You are about to provide difficult and sensitive feedback to one of your most valuable and highest-performing direct reports.	"He is going to take this really hard."	You beat around the bush, couching your feedback with numerous qualifiers. You overemphasize the positives and flatter the direct report.	You appear overly empathetic and vague.	Supportive voice	Your direct report leaves feeling good, a little confused by what the meeting was about, and likely to make the same mistakes again.

TABLE 2-2

John's Signature Voice roadmap: Three levels of conditioning

ACE model	Conditioning	From . . . Baseline ACE	To . . . Signature Voice
Assumptions	Mental conditioning: What is my mind-set?	• Assumed success was about being a great team player within the partnership	• Realize that supporting the partner team actually means leading and driving it • Understand the importance of putting a stake in the ground on what's next and advocating for it with the other partners
Communication strategies and skills	Technical and skill conditioning: What do I say?	• Openly processed thoughts out loud before making decision • Overused core strengths of listening and asking questions in driving for consensus	• Take a strong stand on decisions and communicate consistently and through multiple platforms • Balance out communication style to be more assertive with other partners
Energy	Physical conditioning: How and where do I show up to others?	• Appeared weary • Appeared flustered • Was not visible enough to broader partner group	• Invest in physical self-care • Put structures in place to help prioritize and manage schedule and capacity • Identify ways to engage broader set of partners

TABLE 2-3

Terri's Signature Voice roadmap: Three levels of conditioning

ACE model	Conditioning	From . . . Baseline ACE	To . . . Signature Voice
Assumptions	Mental conditioning: What is my mind-set?	• Wanted to know: What's in it for my function and career?	• Consider other functions, agendas, and the enterprise when making decisions outside her immediate purview • Seek to understand before acting
Communication strategies and skills	Technical and skill conditioning: What do I say?	• Was clear, direct, and concise • Started most of her sentences with "I"	• Listen and ask more questions • Incorporate others' perspectives in what she says
Energy	Physical conditioning: How and where do I show up to others?	• Came off as strong and overbearing • Was easily annoyed and curt • Sounded like she was always judging	• Convey composure when required • Give less judgmental nonverbal cues

What Is Your Baseline ACE?

This drill helps you create an inventory of your baseline—where you are with ACE now—and gives you clues as to where you'll need to focus to enhance your presence.

1. Pick one of the stakeholders from the drill at the end of chapter 1. Try to choose someone who challenges you and perhaps makes you question your presence. Now, think of a specific situation in which you interacted with that person and your presence slid out of Signature Voice to one of the other quadrants. Put an *X* on the matrix in figure 2-3, marking which quadrant you slid to.

2. Think further about the situation. Try to remember the specific interaction, what you were thinking and feeling at the time, and how your body felt. Recall details about the room or what was said to help you conjure the full experience.

3. Now, describe your presence at the time in terms of your:

    Assumptions: What were you thinking and feeling about the situation? What did you do to prepare? What did you think about the person you were interacting with? What did you presume your role was? Write down your assumptions about yourself, the other person, and the situation.

    _____

    _____

    _____

    Communications strategies: What did you say? Did you listen and ask questions? Did you advocate for your or your function's agenda? Write down how you communicated and what strategies you did or didn't use.

    _____

    _____

    _____

FIGURE 2-3

Your presence quadrants

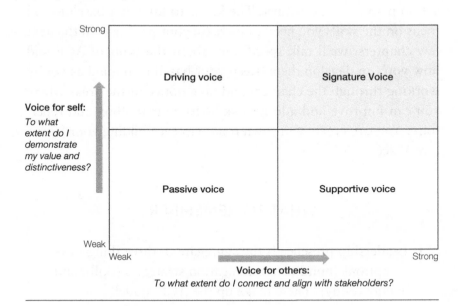

Energy: How did you physically show up in the situation? What was your body language saying? What tone did you set? Write down how you think your body appeared to the other person.

_____

_____

_____

4. Look at what you've written down. Which of the above behaviors and thoughts were serving you well? Which were working against you? What do you think contributed most to your slide out of Signature Voice?

Few of us have the time in our schedules to stop after every interaction we have at work and assess what was going on for us in those moments. However if you take a baseline like the one above you can start to see which thoughts and behaviors are getting in your way. And using the ACE framework, you have a way to notice and categorize what is happening for you.

We notice that many of our clients become energized after doing an initial assessment of ACE because they finally have a clear action plan to work against. The key is to take that baseline and focus on the skills you need to increase your presence. In the next few chapters, we'll talk specifically about the skills of ACE and how you can develop them. Keep your baseline in mind as you're working through the chapters and take notice of the areas where you can improve and add new skills to your toolbox and repertoire. You can create your own roadmap for building your Signature Voice.

WHAT TO REMEMBER

- Leadership presence is the aggregate of three things: assumptions (mind), communication strategies (skill), and energy (body). These make up the ACE model.

- When building your Signature Voice, you need to focus on all three as a system, not just one aspect.

- The ACE model helps you condition your mind, skill, and body for any situation or audience and gives you an actionable way forward that helps you interpret feedback, marries your intent with your desired impact, and honors your strengths.

- While each component of ACE is a separate lever, all three are inextricably linked. Your assumptions drive what you say and how you appear to others. And in return, your communication strategies and energy influence your mind-set.

CHAPTER THREE

ASSUMPTIONS

Mental Conditioning

We start with *assumptions* because they are the bedrock of our words and actions. Your beliefs about yourself, others, and the situation you are in have the power to bolster your presence but also to undermine it. What you think and feel deeply influence your own experience and how other people experience you.

When we sat down with John to work through the feedback he had gotten from his fellow partners—that he was a great team player and that he clearly worked hard to be collaborative and gain consensus—John did not understand what the problem was. Of course, he sought consensus and believed in being a team player. These principles had gotten him far in his career. However, when we went through the feedback in detail, we showed how his assumptions that it was a priority to nurture relationships and maintain harmony with the other firm leaders were not always serving him well. John soon realized these notions were in fact contributing to the rumblings about whether or not he could hold his own as head of North America. How could he do what Roger and the other partners wanted him to—think and act more like a more senior partner—if he was hung up on the fact that he should avoid ruffling any feathers?

At our first meeting with Terri, something similar happened. When we pointed out the assumptions she was making—that there is always a right way to do things—she was defensive. Those beliefs are what gave her confidence and purpose, she argued. They were what drove her to strive for excellence. We pointed to the comments from her peers that showed they thought of Terri as overly focused on *her* agenda and even myopic at times. We explained that unless she was able to build alliances with her peers, she would not get the role she so badly wanted. Terri saw that these assumptions she had made about herself and her role had in fact become roadblocks to her success. (John's and Terri's baseline assumptions and the Signature Voice they wanted to achieve are shown in table 3-1.)

TABLE 3-1

John's and Terri's baseline and Signature Voice assumptions

	JOHN		TERRI	
	Supportive voice	Signature Voice	Driving voice	Signature Voice
Assumptions	• Assumed success was about being a great team player within the partnership	• Realize that supporting the partner team actually means leading and driving it • Understand the importance of putting a stake in the ground on what's next and advocating for it with the other partners	• Wanted to know: What's in it for my function and my career?	• Consider other functions, agendas, and the enterprise when making decisions outside her immediate purview • Seek to understand before acting

To move to Signature Voice, leaders need to question the assumptions they bring to work. John wasn't going to stop believing that being a team player was important. Instead, he needed to reframe that assumption from the perspective of a senior executive with a broader scope of influence. Similarly, Terri had to drop her belief that the most important question was what was in it for her. Both had to replace these outdated assumptions with beliefs that better supported what they were trying to achieve and the leadership presence they wanted to project.

WHY ASSUMPTIONS MATTER

There are countless studies that show that *what you think, believe, and focus on affects what you are able to achieve.*[1] Your assumptions—the ideas and beliefs you hold about yourself and your team, others and their teams, and the terrain and playing field you operate in—become self-fulfilling prophecies. They have a seismic effect on your leadership presence. Negative assumptions—that you do not have what it takes or that you are not senior enough to substantially contribute—can undermine your presence. Positive ones—that you were promoted for good reasons or that you add value to every conversation—make you more confident and bolster your presence.

Like most people, you likely never speak your assumptions out loud; you may not even be aware of their existence. Instead, assumptions stay beneath the surface, a powerful foundation to your every action.

Athletes are familiar with this strong link between thoughts and actions. Across different sports, from college basketball to pro tennis, athletes are regularly coached in how to make the most of their mind-set, to think about their game, their opponents, and what it will take to win. Consider Y.E. Yang, a young South Korean golfer who won his first championship in 2009. He was the first Asian-born player to capture the PGA championship title. Yang started the tournament 5 over par and had a two-shot deficit going into the final round. His final score was 13 under. He did all of this while paired with Tiger Woods, one of the most formidable playing partners and then king of golf. Woods had been 14-0 going into the final round. He had never lost a tournament on American soil when leading by more than one shot. And yet Yang took him down.[2]

As we read the interviews with Yang in the days following the tournament, we were struck by how he articulated his attitude toward Woods. Yang recounted how he put the challenge into perspective, even days before the game: "It's not like you're in an octagon where you're fighting against Tiger and he's going to bite you, or swing at you with his 9-iron," Yang said, speaking through an interpreter. "The worst that I could do was just lose to Tiger. So I really had nothing much at stake."[3] It was this scrappy position that helped Yang to win. He could have just as easily choked under the pressure, ceding the title to Woods because he was the king of golf and Yang wasn't. Instead, Yang refused to accept that assumption and decided he had nothing to lose by playing his best. His confidence, perspective, and clarity helped him to win despite the odds.

The great masters of sports not only have unbelievable skill and are in great physical condition, but they also have mental focus. They have cultivated a mind-set that allows them to overcome doubts, take risks, and put their best selves on the court, the field, or in the rink.

Similarly, examining your beliefs and choosing where to focus your mental energy is a fundamental step to attaining Signature Voice. You need to have your assumptions in check. You may be guided by beliefs that are outdated, inaccurate, left over from a previous role or experience, or simply dead wrong. In this case, your assumptions might be betraying, rather than supporting you. It's not just about positive or negative thinking but about whether what you believe is in line with the reality of the situation.

This chapter addresses three of the most critical assumptions you need to pay attention to enhance your leadership presence:

- *Confidence:* What you bring to the table

- *Perspective:* What hat you wear

- *Clarity:* What your values are

These assumptions are especially critical when you're taking on a larger role or increasing your visibility as a leader. The key is to recognize the assumption you are making, what quadrant you slide to as a result of that assumption, and then to reframe or reset the assumption so that you can get back to Signature Voice. You are going to have beliefs about yourself, those around you, and the situations you are in. You need to make the most of them while preventing them from eroding your presence.

CONFIDENCE: WHAT YOU BRING TO THE TABLE

Meet Tony

Tony was still reveling in his recent promotion to vice president of Sales. The promotion was a significant milestone in his personal career, and Tony was both proud and humbled. He had started out in the field fifteen years ago, selling the company's office supplies directly to retail customers. He was a standout sales rep, and the VP of Sales at the time quickly asked him to lead the Eastern region. In that role, he transformed the area from one of the poorest-performing to number-one in sales.

The CEO, Steve, had watched Tony grow over the years, grooming him and providing advice along the way. Steve was adamant that Tony was ready to lead the sales function he had worked so hard in for over a decade. This recent promotion meant that Tony now had a team of 160 sales representatives and five regional sales directors that reported to him. This group respected his track record and appreciated that he had done his time in the trenches. In his first all-hands meeting with them, he made sure to explain that he was the same Tony he had always been, that they should see him as a peer as much as a leader.

Now, at the executive committee meeting, Tony was proud to be sitting at the table with his new group of peers—the other functional heads for the company: the president, the VP of Operations, the VP of Finance, and the VP of Marketing and Strategy. They were a seasoned team of professionals, many of whom already had decades of experience under their belts.

Before the meeting, Steve explained to Tony that he needed to change how he was perceived. He needed to "step up to the plate," showing that he was a peer to the other executive committee members rather than a former direct report. He told him: "You can't come into this job as a souped-up version of your former self. You need to broaden who you are and convey to everyone above, below, and across from you that you are head of sales now and a key part of my leadership team."

As Tony listened to the other functional heads discuss updates to the year's forecast, he noticed he was holding back. He had things to contribute but couldn't quite find his footing to speak up and engage in the discussion the way the others were. Instead, he felt hamstrung by Steve's advice and his own natural deference to those who had been superior to him just a month before. Looking around the table, he was struck by level of organizational acumen and rigorous debate and he wondered, "I'm just a sales rep. Why am I at the table?"

Why Are You at the Table?

Like many people who have recently made a leadership transition, Tony was about to make a classic mistake: *wrongly assessing what value he was bringing to the table*. Because he was new to the role and the least experienced executive committee member in the room, he assumed that his contributions were of lower value relative to what everyone else offered. In this particular meeting, he was deferring to the other functional heads and ignoring his own thoughts and ideas, which could have helped shape the conversation. His presence slid into supportive voice; he was focusing too heavily on others and not bringing his own voice for self to bear. Tony could have sabotaged his success by making these false—and limiting—assumptions about the value he brought. To move forward, he needed to revisit his beliefs about how he filled his new role and redefine his value proposition. Perhaps it made sense for Tony to hang back as the newest member of the team in this first meeting, but he couldn't remain deferential indefinitely. Steve had promoted him for a reason (probably many reasons). He clearly believed that Tony brought something to the table that was valuable, different, and complementary. And as Steve said, Tony was expected to contribute at a new level.

While this assumption—that you don't bring enough to the table—most often impacts those leaders who need to strengthen their voice for self, those who slide to driving voice need to watch out as well. They tend to operate from a belief that is the opposite of Tony's: they assume that what they bring to the table is always of *highest* value, and they end up standing in the way of others. Their presence feels larger than necessary and overshadows others, blocking their contributions. We've worked with numerous clients who believe that expertise or experience grants them the right to have the loudest voice at the table.

To mentally condition yourself for Signature Voice, you must have a realistic, grounded understanding of what you bring to the table. This is easier said than done. When we work with clients on this endeavor, we warn them that they need to be prepared to explore their strengths, the range of their experiences, and the leadership lessons they've learned to date. It requires a hard look at your past to see what or who has shaped your beliefs about authority and how you define value.

CONFIDENCE: ACTION STEPS

While it's tempting to jump right into defining your value proposition, it's important to first understand your relationship to authority and your beliefs about other people around the table, especially those at the top. When we work with our clients, it's often a specific situation or meeting that has brought this assumption to the surface, such as Tony's promotion, or a meeting with the board, or an interaction with a senior executive that didn't go as intended.

We have heard many tenured, seasoned leaders privately share that even with all the years of experience they have under their belts, they still experience discomfort around the most senior levels of management. They know others would be shocked to hear this. When we ask for more background, we learn that these clients often started out their careers in organizations where a command-and-control leadership style was the norm, or they made critical mistakes in the presence of senior management early in their careers that have left them gun-shy even today. We must address our personal narrative around the *voice for others*, particularly at the very top, before we can confidently define our *voice for self* in the fullest way.

Check Your Authority Story

We all have feelings about authority, no matter what level we are. Some have made it up the ranks questioning authority; others believe deference to seniority is a critical part of any job. You might fall on either end of the spectrum or somewhere in between. Whatever your beliefs, they were formed at a critical juncture in your life: through interactions with your parents, teachers, colleagues, and bosses. Everything you learned along the way has shaped your *authority story*—what you believe about those in charge and your relationship to them (see "Understanding Your Authority Story"). The key is to develop a deeper understanding of your own narrative so that you can recognize how these beliefs affect your presence.

Tony had made his way through the ranks of the sales organization by listening intently to his superiors, heeding their advice, and seeking out their guidance. He was a strong believer that those in charge were in charge for a reason. So when Steve counseled him to present himself as a peer to the other functional

UNDERSTANDING YOUR AUTHORITY STORY

Ask yourself the following questions to better understand your natural tendencies toward authority and hierarchies:

- Do you believe that hierarchies should be a thing of the past—that they are little more than lines on an organization chart?

- Do you believe that the best ideas can come from anyone in the room, regardless of tenure, experience, expertise, or title?

- Do you believe that hierarchies serve an important purpose?

heads and as a leader to his former peers, he was uncomfortable. What gave him the right to assume this new position of power? This authority story was working against him in two ways. First, with his new peers, his natural deference was keeping him from fully participating in critical strategic discussions that would impact the team and the organization. Second, with his new team, he was hesitant to step up and plant the flag as their new leader. Tony was working harder than before to still be one of the team, hoping to make everyone, including himself, feel comfortable. He hadn't defined his voice for self in this new role.

It was time for Tony to reframe what *authority* meant so that he could make the contributions he needed to as an executive. To increase his voice in the room in an authentic way, Tony had to reset his assumption. We coached Tony to let go of his deference to authority and replace it with something he could also believe in: an *appropriate respect for seniority while holding his own new power*.

This is a critical step for people like Tony or John to strengthen their voice as leaders. But an authority story is just as important

WHAT IS TERRI'S AUTHORITY STORY?

By taking a closer look at her own feelings about authority, Terri realized that she thrived most in situations where she was the authority in the room. She liked to be in charge. She felt at her best when she was providing monthly updates to the senior management team on her functional area because she always had a strong command of her business area. She flourished when working with her team because there was a clear chain of command with her at the top and no ambiguity about who had the authority to make decisions. When Terri took on her new position as the lead for her company's cross-functional task force, she could no longer rely on the chain of command. Success in this new role required that she influence without formal authority. This was a new ball game for Terri. She needed to understand how her assumption about being the most powerful or in-command person in the room could hold her back.

---

for someone like Terri. (See "What Is Terri's Authority Story?" on how she worked through her own assumptions.)

For someone like Terri, who needs to strengthen her voice for others, it's important that she retain her natural comfort around those in senior leadership positions while also adding more of a voice for others when interacting with her peer executives.

One of our clients, Barbara, is a great example of the strength you can gain from clarity on your relationship to authority. As a newly elected partner in an executive search firm, she recounted her experience of attending her first partner meeting and finally having a seat at the table she had worked so hard to reach. Barbara had never been one to shy away from sharing her opinions. When she was up for partner, she felt confident in the contributions and value add she had brought the firm to date. And at this first official partners meeting, she was conscious that she would make contributions to the discussion and not sit silent.

She was, however, equally mindful of the voices of those who had sat at that same table for years preceding her. In some instances, while she had an opinion, she made the conscious decision to not speak up in the room but to raise issues with her new peers afterward. She was savvy enough to discern which areas of the discussion were potential landmines and know that if she were to raise those issues, she might catch others off guard in front of the rest of the partnership. Barbara demonstrated the agility with voice for self and others in a way that allowed her to say what she needed to while being appropriately respectful to her fellow partners.

Whatever your authority story, it's important to get to know it before defining what value you bring to the table. Let's be realistic: in today's business world, hierarchy is not irrelevant. Most organizations, even those that claim to be flat, have unspoken rules and norms about authority. Only you know your organization's cultural norms. But what's important is that you don't let your beliefs hijack you, either by unconsciously sitting back or overpowering the key players around the table.

Once you've adopted an authority story that serves you, it's time to take a look at what value you bring to the table. Understanding your value proposition is a critical component to building a strong, healthy voice for self. Further, it helps to prioritize your time and efforts and helps others understand what they can count on you for.

Define Your Value Proposition

Again, getting to a clear understanding of your value proposition can be challenging. It requires looking at the unique combination of strengths, skills, experience, passions, and preferences you bring to your role. Your value proposition is a key part of the word *signature* in Signature Voice. You gain clarity on your vision as a leader when you discern and articulate the value you bring. This is especially important to do in new roles, but it is also valuable to take a closer look at your value proposition in the role you're currently filling, no matter how long you've been in it. Take time to pull back from the day-to-day and assess where and how you can provide the highest value. Ask yourself:

- What are my unique strengths, and what do I contribute that others don't?

- What is the scope of my role and my sphere of influence?

- What does success look like in my role?

KNOW YOUR UNIQUE STRENGTHS. A key element of your value proposition is the strengths you bring to your role or organization, especially those that others don't. Identifying the unique spikes in your skills builds your confidence and keeps you engaged in your role and position. The Gallup organization conducted a forty-year study on human strengths that indicates that "people who do have the opportunity to focus on their strengths every day are six times as likely to be engaged in their jobs and three times as likely to report having an excellent quality of life in general."[4] For Terri, there is no doubt that her drive for results, strategic agility, and innovation are what she uniquely contributes to her organization. Knowing that allows her to be sure she is always in roles that engage these skills. Ask yourself: What are your greatest strengths? What is it that you are able to do that others can't? Think back to your previous jobs: Which ones gave you the most energy? Which ones felt effortless? What unique strengths did you bring to those roles? Validate your own instincts around your natural talents and strengths by looking at 360 feedback or asking trusted colleagues what they most appreciate about what you bring to the table.

APPROPRIATELY SIZE YOUR ROLE AND SPHERE OF INFLUENCE. Your assumptions about the size of your role and sphere of influence can have tremendous impact on presence. Many individuals define their roles too narrowly or rigidly. One of our clients, Samantha, a VP at an investment management firm, articulated her role in maximizing returns in the managed portfolio as "taking the hill." This motivated her to see the challenge in front of her with each investment and tackle it. However, when we sat with her and discussed what it was she did with each of the investments, she realized that the changes she pushed through had large strategic implications and required involvement from the senior-most managing directors at the firm. She realized her job was to see and win the *war*, not just take single hills. The metaphor of taking the hill was actually limiting her ability to have a broader impact. By updating her assumption to match the true scope of her role—to think about "winning the battlefield"—she was able to be more assertive about her work. She brought a whole new level of confidence and natural gravitas when speaking with the managing directors in her firm about what was happening across the portfolio.

It's possible to do the opposite as well. Another client of ours, Alec, was a VP of Finance for a global software company. He dominated every meeting he was in with endless monologues on what he deemed important information. It was clear from listening to him that he held a conviction that all roads stemmed from and led back to Finance. According to him, his function was the hub of the company. He assumed that because he had the most knowledge on the topic and that his function was critical, others should listen to his views. Alec's presence was in driving voice. It was no exaggeration that he was an expert in his field, and he often said important—even brilliant—things. But people failed to hear them because he never made it about them or acknowledged their value. As a result, they'd learned to tune him out.

Where Samantha had undervalued her role, Alec had overvalued his. The key is to better understand what the true scope of your position is.

This kind of mental conditioning is especially important during transitions. Recently, we heard Winston, the COO of a consumer products company, recount this story to a group of high-potentials attending one of our executive education programs:

I started my career as an operations analyst, as many of you probably did. And after a few years of being heads down and delivering good work, I was chosen to become a manager—not because I had managed well; in fact, I had never managed at all. I was promoted because I was the best analyst in the group. Despite my lack of knowledge, I somehow figured out how to be a decent manager. I did what I knew best: I passed on my technical knowledge to my team. Not too long after, I was tapped as the leader of the information systems group, an area where I had absolutely no technical expertise. If I didn't have managerial skills and I didn't have the right expertise, what was I doing there? At that point, I had to really look at myself and ask, "How do I add value here?"

Winston realized when he took on the new position that the assumptions he had made about what he was good at and what he brought to the table needed to change. In asking himself these questions, Winston was recalibrating his understanding of what would make him most effective in his new role. He would have failed if he had assumed that how he added value as the lead of the systems group was the same way he had added value as an operations analyst and operations manager. Instead, he paused at this inflection point to determine the scope of his new role and changed his mind-set accordingly.

DEFINE SUCCESS. The definition of success in any role is a combination of what you believe is required and what the organization deems is required. Leaders often presume that they know what their boss or colleagues expect from the role. This can be a dangerous assumption. It's critical that you see eye to eye with those around you, especially your superiors, on what success means in your role. Tony, the newly promoted VP of Sales, was somewhat surprised to find out his colleagues expected him to bring a fresh set of eyes and leadership perspective to the table and not his deference to their authority. In fact, when he took the back seat in conversations, assuming that his peers preferred to have the floor, it frustrated them. They felt Tony was being too submissive and disengaged. Tony's success hinged on his ability to contribute as a peer but he realized this only after hearing the feedback from Steve. Don't assume you know your stakeholders' expectations—ask. And don't assume they know your expectations and vision for the job—share and discuss with them what success looks like.

Consider Francis Collins, the director of the National Institutes of Health. In the summer of 2009, he was nominated to the role by President Obama, and the Senate unanimously confirmed him. After a break from leading one unit of the NIH, the Human Genome Project, he returned to become the head of all twenty-three institutes. This required a fundamental shift in his vision of himself as a leader. He could no longer be aligned with the popular Genome Project; he now had to shift his attention to the broad portfolio of the NIH. It was important that in this new role, his stakeholders understand that his commitment wasn't to where he came from but to the entire organization. Since the institutes all compete for funding, he had to be careful not to display any bias. At his first all-hands meeting with the over eighteen thousand employees of the NIH, Collins shared his vision as a leader of their organization. He described himself as a "conductor of the orchestra, focused on choosing the scores."[5] This was an authentic metaphor for Collins, given his background as a musician, but also a way of conveying that what was required of him in this new role was fundamentally different. He reframed for himself and the organization the assumptions about success.

For Terri and John, defining why they were at the table proved powerful in enhancing their leadership presence. In fact, Terri didn't lose her strong voice for self—it was her signature, after all. Instead, she reset her assumptions and set a new course for herself as a leader. She went from thinking of herself as "the prima donna quarterback" to thinking and acting like the "head coach" of the cross-functional team. This new assumption helped her to focus on the team and less on herself. John also didn't lose his strong voice for others—he simply shifted his assumption about what made him successful (see "How Did John Reset His Assumptions?"). He set a new vision for himself: he was no longer an "of-

HOW DID JOHN RESET HIS ASSUMPTIONS?

Through 360-feedback interviews, John learned more about how others perceived him. Senior partners at the firm described him as warm, trustworthy, and approachable. They thought he was a fantastic leader for the Chicago office but did not view him as someone who could effectively corral all of the partners and their differing agendas in a broader role. In coaching, we focused on the concept of being a "firm owner and leader" rather than just an "office manager." This vision resonated for John because it spoke to the part of him that was naturally comfortable being in service to others and his strong sense of commitment to something larger. But it also raised the bar on the type of leadership he could offer. He wasn't in the room to just observe and speak up when it was relevant for the Chicago office but had to make his voice heard on firmwide issues and recommend a pathway forward. This required he shift from a peer partner mind-set to a lead partner mind-set.

fice leader and supporter of others"; he needed to be a "driver and leader of the entire firm." This emboldened him to assert himself more with other partners and put a stake in the ground on key decisions.

DRILL

Update Your Bio

When we work with clients, we don't let them stop at articulating a clear value proposition or personal brand statement. In order to make it concrete and actionable, we ask them to translate their newly articulated value proposition into real deliverables. One of our favorite exercises is asking clients to update their bios. This may seem like an uninteresting chore, but it forces leaders to review their accomplishments and experiences and bring them into a focused, relevant format that clearly demonstrates what they bring to the table. When Terri and John pulled up the most recent version of their bios, they found outdated versions of themselves. They then used the opportunity to reflect on their unique strengths, the scope of their current roles, and what success meant to them now.

Find your most recent bio. Read through it and think about how you would describe yourself at this moment. Answer each of the questions below:

1. If I had to describe my value proposition in three key messages, what would I say?

2. What three pieces of information should I include to make my areas of expertise clear?

3. What three pieces of information should I include so that others know how to position me for new roles that allow me bring my highest value to the organization?

Once you have answers to the above, you can put them into different formats that you can immediately put to use. Here are three versions of your bio that you should have ready:

- A one-minute and three-minute elevator pitch about yourself

- A speaker's bio to provide when you're invited to speak at industry or organization conferences

- A public bio that can be used in marketing proposals or other situations when your organization is meeting with an external entity

One of our clients, a newly minted CFO for an insurance company, pulled up his bio and was shocked how much it read like a "corporate reporter/bean counter." In his new bio, he included messages about how he formed strategic partnerships with the business.

Another client at a technology consulting firm updated his outdated and generic bio, which listed a myriad of projects, to a much more thoughtful bio that highlighted his particular success developing the firm business in emerging technologies. The very act of rewriting it boosted his voice for self!

PERSPECTIVE: WHAT HAT YOU WEAR

Meet Kathy

Kathy could feel her blood pressure rise when it was time for questions. This was the first meeting of a one-month road show to provide the latest update on the rollout of a new, enterprisewide purchasing software. It had been a controversial software decision, but as the senior director of IT, Kathy had pushed it forward, ultimately winning the green light from the senior leadership team, largely because of her in-depth knowledge about the product and her compelling argument for how it would benefit the enterprise. Kathy knew the new software would ensure that purchasing data was collected in a more consistent, harmonized way across all lines of business. But now, at her very first meeting, people were asking what she considered to be irrelevant questions. *How were they not getting it?* she wondered.

She had prepared for every question she could think of: the specifics of the rollout team, detailed timelines, the ins and outs of the system architecture and infrastructure. She had personally made sure that she was deeply involved in every stage of development and knew the software and the implementation plans like the back of her hand.

But now her counterparts were asking senseless questions, and she was extremely frustrated. It was as if they didn't care about the new functionality or the benefits everyone stood to gain in the long run. They wanted to know how long it would take to learn the system, how much time their people would spend in training, and who would help with questions. They seemed dead set on undermining the whole project because they didn't want to be inconvenienced by having to learn a new system. Kathy felt attacked. Defensively, she continued to repeat the key points from the slides she had prepared.

What Perspective Are You Holding?

Kathy knows her stuff. She is a functional leader and has skills and expertise that are impressive and valuable. But she is so focused on her voice for self that she's no longer aware of the others in the room. Her presence has slid to driving voice. She sees the world through the lens of her function only and assumes that what is good for her function will be good for everyone else. This assumption is perilous because it alienates others.

In Kathy's case, she wrongly assumed that her colleagues would see the world from her own perspective. She thought they should take her word at face value and see the system as a benefit, not an inconvenience. She walked into that meeting with her "IT hat" on and failed to see things from the perspective of her audience, the overall leadership team. She was now struggling to gain buy-in for a project she cared deeply about.

Shifting your presence to Signature Voice requires you to take a broader perspective. You are on the road to becoming an enterprise leader, and it's never too early to begin thinking like one. Keep the functional hat that you are comfortable with, but also practice wearing a more strategic, organization-focused hat to give you the wider purview.

Ram Charan, Stephen Drotter, and James Noel make this point beautifully in *The Leadership Pipeline*: "Maturity involves thinking like a businessperson rather than just a functionary . . . being able to consider how a decision impacts not only one's community but also the larger society of which one is a member . . ."[6] As you go through each leadership passage, you need to be preparing for the next. And you can't wait until the day you receive your

C-level or managing director title to start thinking like one. You need to begin honing your ability to take an organization-wide view early on. Here's how.

PERSPECTIVE: ACTION STEPS

There are several steps you can take to broaden your perspective. These include trying on other hats to see issues through others' eyes and taking a broader, more strategic view.

Try On Other Hats

But wait a minute. Didn't we just suggest you spend time on defining your value proposition and how you add value? The functional and technical expertise you bring to the organization is what makes you valuable to your function, what's likely driven a good deal of your success to date, and is the foundation for your perspective. But as you pursue your career, there comes a time when you must expand your perspective beyond your immediate area of expertise and look up, down, and sideways.

To move towards the leadership maturity that Charan, Drotter, and Noel describe, and to achieve Signature Voice, you must try on other hats. For people like Kathy and Terri, whose presence slides to driving voice, this requires building a fundamental awareness about what's important to other functions and teams. In Kathy's case, she imagined that her cross-functional colleagues would value the same things she did. She hadn't asked herself before the meeting, *What would they care about most?* Instead, she presumed they would agree with her on all points. If Kathy had done the "roadshow before the roadshow" and met with key leaders in advance to understand their concerns, she could have addressed those directly and built consideration for them into her presentation.

Those who are great at negotiations often get a bad rap for looking out for their side only. But the truly skilled negotiators embrace this less intuitive assumption: *you cannot create and optimize value until you understand the perspective of the other parties*. According to William Ury, cofounder of the Harvard Negotiation Project and author of *Getting Past No*, "The single most important skill in negotiation is the ability to put yourself in the other side's shoes. If you are trying to change their thinking, you need to begin by understanding what their thinking is."[7]

Leigh Steinberg, one of the country's leading sports agents (he is often credited as the real-life inspiration for *Jerry Maguire*), was well aware of this. He built an incredible thirty-five-year career representing hundreds of professional athletes in football, baseball, basketball, volleyball, golf, boxing, and Olympic sports. In his book, *Winning with Integrity*, Steinberg says, "Rather than simply dismiss the other party's position entering a negotiation as unrealistic, unfair, and unjustifiable, it is far more fruitful to consider that position from his viewpoint . . . and understand how he could possibly justify his position to himself. Then, you will be in a better position to respond to that justification . . . A key to creating those solutions is the ability to put yourself at every moment into the psyche of this other human being and to be able to somehow fashion a way of fulfilling both sets of goals—yours and his."[8]

In everyday business situations, not just negotiations, it behooves you—and enhances your presence—to try on other hats and see the world from a different perspective. To do this, you need to grasp an issue from all sides. This means actively considering what others will think about the issue, what they have to lose or stand to gain, and what their priorities are. Sometimes this is easier said than done. You may not know what the other party wants, just as Kathy was unclear on what her counterparts cared most about when it came to the new system. But don't let lack of imagination hinder you. Sit down with other functional leaders and find out what they care about. Propose a trade where you share what your area is concerned with and working on and your counterpart can do the same. Attend their all-staff meetings to share the latest from your function and invite them to yours. (For a take on Terri's strategy, see "How Did Terri Broaden Her Perspective?")

HOW DID TERRI BROADEN HER PERSPECTIVE?

When Terri became the lead of the cross-functional initiative, she took to heart the feedback she had received. She realized she would need to think differently about how to engage and enroll her peers. Part of the problem Terri faced was that she tended to view decisions from her perspective. As a result, she was most motivated to advocate for decisions that would benefit her function. This alienated others and pushed her presence further into driving voice. In order to better connect and align with her cross-functional peers, Terri had to realize that her role was to do what was best for her company, not just her function. The only way she could do this was by being open to the other functions' perspectives. Terri made a deliberate decision to try this approach. Before every meeting and at every point where a decision was being made, she conscientiously asked herself, "What is best for the company here?" She also took the time to consider how each of her peers might approach the decision and the impact on each of their areas.

As you listen and observe, try to understand how your function fits into the other agendas. Don't be afraid to ask: How do we stand in your way? Or how can we make your job easier? You may not be able to change those things, but you will gain insight into where your agendas overlap or clash.

Take a Broader, More Strategic View

Trying on another hat does not mean you have to agree with the other function's or person's agenda. In fact, if you compromise your own value to fit their needs, you risk losing your voice for self and your presence sliding to supportive voice. One of our clients, who works in the legal department at an energy company, recently realized that her assumption "I'm a support function serving my internal customers" kept getting in the way of building a strong alliance with her colleagues. She acted as if she was supporting them, rather than partnering with them. We suggested she try shifting her thinking from "I'm a support function; I'm an order taker" to "I'm a strategic partner to the business." This relatively small change in mind-set makes her feel less like a meddling lawyer whom others resented or dreaded interacting with to a valuable contributor serving the business in a critical manner. As a result, her internal customers are reaching out to her more and including her in key strategic decisions.

Being in Signature Voice means you are able to see an issue through a strategic lens. Once you've developed a better understanding of the holistic picture of your organization, you need to make it your operating platform. One of our clients describes this as being able to "helicopter up to the über-goal of the organization." Executives with effective presence do what's best for the organization, even if it's not in the immediate interest of their function. It's essential for leaders to "get on the balcony." Ron Heifetz, Marty Linksy, and Alexander Grashow coined this phrase in their book, *The Practice of Adaptive Leadership*, to suggest that leaders rise above the situation, see the big picture, and get off center stage.[9] Integrate multiple agendas into your decisions. When considering options, put aside your self-interest and try on different hats, building your business acumen and strategic agility along the way. Ask yourself: What would Finance think about the options? What would IT believe is the right solution? Seeing it from all sides will help you get a more robust answer. And the more you act from this broader view, the more you are perceived as an organizational leader, no matter where you sit in the organization. You should be able to articulate why the decision is best for everyone, not just you.

The next time you consider potential solutions to a critical decision, ask yourself:

- How can I put aside my self-interest and stay objective?

- Have I considered the multiple perspectives, positions, and interests at play?

- Have I looked at the issue from an organizational perspective, wearing a strategic hat rather than a functional one?

Adding these questions to your repertoire has two key benefits:

- You strengthen your strategic thinking capabilities.

- You're able to communicate more effectively, especially with your peers and the highest levels of management.

One of our clients had received feedback that she tended to see things through her functional lens. Every response to a question or problem demonstrated that she was thinking about what was best for her function. Even when she agreed with an enterprise-level decision, she always needed to let others know the impact on her group. For example, she'd add at the end of a discussion, "Well, that will certainly require a lot of extra time from my group." To change the perception that she could only think about her function, we asked her to go through the above questions before each meeting. The idea was that she needed to create a new mental model to respond to others. She was better able to explain the decision she supported and how it fit into what was best for the entire organization and its strategic priorities. Then she was able to calmly explain the necessary trade-offs and any potential impact on resources. In some cases, she realized the right thing to do was to advocate for her team, but that was no longer her default. To her surprise, simply reflecting on the questions above made her feel more confident as a senior leader—and increased her reputation as one.

CLARITY: WHAT YOUR VALUES ARE

Meet Eric

Eric returned to his office in Atlanta feeling frustrated and angry. He had spent the past week at a global partners meeting in Zurich, where the accounting firm's leaders had gathered to make several decisions about firm operations, including new performance management standards to be rolled out globally in the coming year. There had been fierce debate about the changes. Eric was most concerned about the proposed alterations to the rating scale. For years, the firm had a detailed scale that allowed managers to make granular distinctions and left room for individual judgment. Stacy, a senior partner from San Francisco, had proposed a pared-down scale that was simpler but, in Eric's view, would stifle development discussions and leave the firm's more junior staff scratching their heads. How would they know what to improve on without the detail that the original scale required? How could Stacy be so irresponsible with the career development of the firm's future generations of leaders?

Now that he was back in the office, Eric felt drained. He was still reeling from the heated interaction with Stacy. Why had she bothered him so much? He was embarrassed by how he had flown off the handle, but he felt he had no choice. She seemed dead set on creating a more user-friendly system and saving the firm money and the partners' time, but at the sacrifice of the staff's development. To Eric, this wasn't a reasonable trade-off. And now he had to figure out how to communicate the new system to the staff. He knew he had to present a unified front with the rest of the partnership but he didn't know how he was going to do that. He was too angry with Stacy and the other partners who went along with her proposal. At moments like this, he questioned whether the firm was the right place for him as a senior leader.

What Matters to You?

At the deepest level of assumptions are core values, those things that matter most to each individual. When you feel aligned to your values, you feel energized and thrive. And, conversely, when these values are offended or violated, you feel drained and frustrated. Getting in touch with your values and understanding how they impact presence is critical to sustaining a Signature Voice.

Eric clearly cared deeply about the development of staff, and Stacy had gotten under his skin by advocating for a change that he felt would jeopardize the firm's commitment to that value. Eric had some valid points. Development of people is critical to any firm's future. And it might be unfair to shortchange the staff, if that is what the new system will indeed do. But the issue is not about whether Eric is "right." The question is what is best for the firm and whether Eric can live with the answer.

The real problem is that Eric doesn't recognize that this is why he is so upset. His presence slid to driving voice, where he got hung up on his own viewpoint and was unable to see or appreciate that of others. The slide in Eric's presence was caused by his perception that his values were being violated. There are two common reactions when your values are threatened. Some, like Eric and Terri, lean heavily on their voice for self when challenged and judge those who are proposing what they think is unfair or unjust. Others, like John, whose presence slides to supporting voice, begin to feel like victims. They believe people are out to get them and tend to blame others for their own inability to speak up.

The tricky thing about values is that they are individual to each person. You can't assume that others will have the same values as you. Instead, you need to acknowledge that while different, others' values are equally important. Figure 3-1 shows the assumptions you are likely to make, depending on which quadrant your presence has slid to.

These assumptions can be dangerous, as they jeopardize your connection with those around you and can erode your self-confidence. On the flip side, when you know what your values are—what you are willing to stand for—and can accept that others don't hold the same ones, your values can be a source of strength. Values are often demonstrated through one's words, actions, responses, and decisions and often indicate the type of culture a leader will thrive leading in or how he or she will shape or create the culture as a leader. They bolster your voice, giving you a platform from which to speak and act. (See how John did this in "John Uses Values to Bolster His Presence.")

FIGURE 3-1

Assumptions you are likely to make

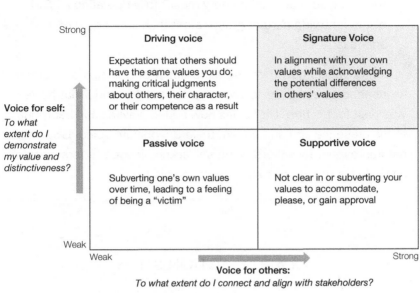

Voice for self:
To what extent do I demonstrate my value and distinctiveness?

Strong

Driving voice	Signature Voice
Expectation that others should have the same values you do; making critical judgments about others, their character, or their competence as a result	In alignment with your own values while acknowledging the potential differences in others' values

Passive voice	Supportive voice
Subverting one's own values over time, leading to a feeling of being a "victim"	Not clear in or subverting your values to accommodate, please, or gain approval

Weak

Weak ———————————> Strong

Voice for others:
To what extent do I connect and align with stakeholders?

JOHN USES VALUES TO BOLSTER HIS PRESENCE

For John, identifying and uncovering his values was an important way to increase his voice for self. Rather than making decisions based on popular consensus, he learned to use his values as a guide for decision making and taking action. As he reflected on what mattered most to him, he identified the following:

1. *Quality:* By focusing on this value, John found he was able to hold a stronger line when he felt that other partners were not pulling their weight. Instead of shying away from confrontation, he felt emboldened to help them improve, even if it meant providing tough feedback.

2. *Honesty:* John realized that when he subjugated his own voice for self, he was being dishonest with others. By focusing on honesty as a core value, he gained the courage to more forthrightly share his views.

3. *Teaming:* At heart, John was a team player. Working and col-
laborating with others was important to him, but he reframed
this value so that teaming now meant fully operating as part
of the firmwide partner group rather than supporting others'
agendas.

John's values gave him the extra boost of managerial courage
he needed to stand up for what he believed in and what he felt
was best for his firm. His values now added gravitas and backbone
to his presence and shifted him toward Signature Voice. Given his
natural respect for others, John still acknowledged others' values
but held his ground by being clearer on his own.

CLARITY: ACTION STEPS

To leverage your values in a positive way, understand your hot
buttons—those things that matter most to you. Then, let go of the
notion that you can convince others of your values and instead
focus on what you have in common.

Understand Your Hot Buttons

If everyone you worked with held the same values as you, projects
would go more smoothly, you would effortlessly reach alignment
on priorities, and discussions would wrap up in a matter of minutes. But, of course, this is completely unrealistic. Instead, there
will likely be moments when the people you work with violate the
principles that matter most to you.

You need to find a way to deal with it when it occurs. Start by
understanding what values you hold most near and dear. In our
work with Eric, he reflected on times in his career when he was
in Signature Voice and realized that at those moments two values were at play: fairness and rigor. When he understood things

were fair and based on merit, he felt motivated to perform at his personal best. When he perceived that his team had done the appropriate analysis and diligence in problem solving, he felt at ease and able to perform. On the other hand, when those values were violated or missing, his presence shifted to driving voice, where he became highly critical of others.

With this awareness, he could see how the new rating system hit a nerve for him, and why he was so angry with Stacy. We then encouraged him to think about what values Stacy cared about most. Thinking about how she articulated the business case for the new system, Eric understood that Stacy valued simplicity and efficiency. This allowed him to admit that Stacy wasn't "wrong" for pushing the system but that she was putting a different value—efficiency—first.

The point here is not to give up on your values. Eric doesn't need to compromise on his belief in fairness and rigor. But by recognizing the conflict, he could avoid the emotional charge and the slide to driving voice. He could be more objective and put on his strategic hat. He came to appreciate that streamlining the process and setting up more consistent standards could help the firm—and ultimately, were in line with his value of fairness.

Even more important, he recognized that while he had lost the battle around the rating system, he didn't have to stop caring about the development of his people. He eventually collaborated with Stacy to create guidelines and training for the new system that ensured that people still had rigorous discussions with their direct reports that went beyond what the system required.

Focus on the Common Goal

Instead of trying to convince those around you that they should believe in the same values as you, focus on what you have in common. Usually this is a shared goal. Stacy was concerned about the financial health of the firm and how much time partners dedicated to internal systems and processes. Eric was worried that future

generations of leaders weren't going to get the input and feedback they needed to be successful. Stacy and Eric were at odds
when they focused on these differences. Instead, they needed to
pay attention to what they had in common: the ultimate health
and growth of the firm.

Uncovering assumptions around values helps individuals better
understand what motivates them, what defines success, and what
ultimately gives meaning to their lives. As leaders explore their
assumptions, they inevitably question their own values. After all,
they are at the heart of voice for self.

Uncovering one's values is not an easy task. When asked "What
are your values?" clients tend to go blank. It's more helpful to
look at a list of words and then think about concrete situations
when certain values were at play. You may find you have to go
through this exercise a few times to really narrow your list.

DRILL

Align Your Values to Your Signature Voice

1. Look at the list of words shown in table 3-2.

2. Now think about times in your career when you were most
   energized, inspired, and in your Signature Voice. Cross out the
   values that don't resonate with those feelings.

3. Continue to cross out words until you have five remaining. You'll
   likely have to make some tough choices at the end but you'll
   discover the five that most resonate with you.

4. Now, based on your actions, behaviors, and decisions, select
   five words *others* would use to describe how you lead. Are they
   the same as the ones above?

5. Which five words reflect how you would *like to* lead and have
   others use to describe how you lead? Again, compare with the
   two sets you just created.

TABLE 3-2

Values list

Accountability	Excellence	Mission
Achievement	Expertise	Open-mindedness
Adaptability	Fairness/equality	Organizational growth
Ambition	Family	Passion
Autonomy	Financial stability	Patience
Balance (work/home)	Flexibility	Performance
Beauty	Formality	Personal growth
Caution	Freedom	Positive attitude
Challenge	Friendship	Power
Clarity	Generosity	Productivity
Coaching/mentoring	Happiness	Professional growth
Commitment	Health	Professionalism
Community involvement	Hard work	Quality
Compassion	Hierarchy	Recognition
Competence	Honesty/integrity	Respect
Conflict resolution	Hope	Resilience
Continuous learning	Human rights	Responsibility
Consensus	Humility	Reward
Cooperation	Humor/fun	Security
Courage	Inclusiveness	Risk-taking
Creativity	Informality	Safety
Curiosity	Information sharing	Simplicity
Customer satisfaction	Initiative	Social responsibility
Decisiveness	Innovation	Spirituality/faith
Dependability	Intelligence	Strength
Discipline	Interdependence	Success
Diversity	Knowledge	Teamwork
Efficiency	Leaving a legacy	Transparency
Effectiveness	Listening	Trust
Empathy	Logic	Truth
Enthusiasm	Long-term perspective	Vision
Entrepreneurism	Loyalty	Wealth
Environmental awareness	Making a difference	Well-being

Clients often complete this exercise excited by what they uncover. They recount experiences of leading with their core values and describe how energized and invigorated they were in those situations. Many aren't aware of the values that were at play. Other clients gain a lot from considering their "aspirational" values: how they hope to lead and the legacy they aspire to leave. One client who worked hard to strengthen his voice for others and manage his slide to driving voice wondered what it would mean to add open-mindedness to the things he valued. Could he use that value to guide his future work inspiring teams?

DRILL

Your Assumptions

In this chapter, we've addressed the three critical assumptions leaders need to pay attention to—especially when taking on a bigger role where the importance of presence increases—and how you can reset them so they are working for you rather than against you. Table 3-3 lists some of the most common assumptions executives make:

TABLE 3-3

Common assumptions and how to reset them

Assumption	Quadrant your presence ends up in	The *new* assumption
Confidence: **What you bring to the table**		
I don't have enough experience to meaningfully contribute.	Supportive	I have enough experience in my particular area of expertise to contribute to the overall picture.
People should value my expertise and knowledge.	Driving	My expertise combined with others' knowledge will get us the best possible outcome.
Perspective: **What hat you wear**		
I have to ensure all perspectives are taken into account to maintain harmony.	Supportive	I have to consider all perspectives, while also articulating and holding my own, to ultimately determine what's best for the enterprise.
My perspective supports what's best for all.	Driving	I have to be open to others' perspectives to truly do what's best for everyone.
Clarity: **What your values are**		
What I care about does not seem relevant to them.	Supportive	We have different values but we care about the same goals, and it's my responsibility to articulate what matters to me.
What they care about is not relevant/helpful/important to our goals.	Driving	We can get to the goal while honoring and respecting everyone's values.

WHAT TO REMEMBER

- Looking at the assumptions you make is important because they underscore every action you take and word you speak. They are the foundation from which you act. Any cracks or faults in this base will have ripple effects throughout your behavior and can undermine your best intentions. For many, tacit assumptions are unnecessary baggage that holds them back.

- To mentally condition your Signature Voice, you need to continually update your assumption of what you bring to the table. Being clear on your value proposition—knowing your personal brand and vision for yourself as a leader—is a key component of mental confidence.

- Your perspective influences your presence. As you become more senior, you need to think at the level of the organization rather than restricting your view to a function or unit. By taking a strategic perspective, you can better align and coordinate other groups and functions.

- Your values can either bolster your presence or get in your way. Gain clarity on your hot buttons—know what matters most to you while acknowledging that others have different values.

CHAPTER FOUR

COMMUNICATION STRATEGIES
Skill Conditioning

Now that you've thought through how to address and re-set your assumptions for Signature Voice, it's time to turn your attention to the second component of the ACE model: *communication strategies.* What you say and how you say it play a large role in creating an effective presence and are an important part of conditioning for Signature Voice. While assumptions help to increase confidence, make clear our value proposition, and give conviction to our values, communication strategies increase our ability to be adaptive. A leader with a full communications reper-toire can have an effective presence in a variety of situations. Your communication strategies are one of the first ways that people perceive you. Based on what you say, they make judgments about your presence and your competence as a leader. Therefore, this is where you often gain the most traction with your presence. Here you need to ask yourself: What communication strategies or skills will help me enhance my presence and impact?

In an interview with the *New York Times*, Amy Schulman, executive vice president, global counsel, and president of Nutrition at Pfizer highlighted the importance of having a well-rounded set of communication strategies. When asked about the biggest leadership lessons she's learned, she said:

> *One of the biggest lessons I'm learning now is having a better feel for when to step out of a situation and when to step in. I do think that is actually one of the hardest things to balance correctly. People want to hear from you. They want your opinion. And if you don't ever speak up and weigh in, then I think the people you lead will feel frustrated, wondering why you're hanging back and not saying what you think. But if you're constantly giving direction and speaking, then you're really not encouraging conversation. And no matter how democratic you'd like to think you are as a boss, you learn that your voice is louder than others' . . . I think learning to refrain from speaking—without making people feel that you're trying to frustrate them by being opaque—has been an inflection point for me . . . It was just watching the room, and being puzzled if I thought there should be conversation, and wondering why there wasn't more conversation. I also saw how quickly people tended to agree with me, so I thought, it can't be that I'm right all this time. And so I learned to really try to deliberately reward people in a conversation for challenging me. I don't mean being insubordinate. I mean really following up on other people's ideas. One of the marks of a good speaker is actually being a great listener. So I remind myself that no matter how quick I think I am, that I have to show that I'm listening, and show people how I've gotten to the endpoint, or else I run the risk of squelching conversation. So I will deliberately slow myself down so that the room catches up to where I am. I know how I feel when I get cut off, and so shame on me if I do that to other people.[1]*

Schulman has learned to be adaptive and to use the communication strategies required for each unique situation. She is balancing her voice for self and her voice for others when she decides whether to speak up or hold back.

When Roger gave John feedback about why he might not be considered for managing partner, he pointed to John's communication skills as an occasional weakness. He explained that John often allowed himself to get flustered by the internal politics of a situation and seemed to backpedal during tough conversations, starting with one opinion but then changing his position over the course of the discussion. This left the senior partners with the impression that he hadn't thought through his viewpoint beforehand. John thought he was being flexible and adaptable, taking others' opinions into account. Roger shared that, as a senior leader at the firm, John needed to put more of a stake in the ground when it came to firm issues. He felt that John lacked consistency in his messages, which in turn allowed others to drive things according to their own agendas. Roger explained that he would engender a lot more support if he demonstrated more firmness and forethought when speaking.

Those in Terri's world saw her communications skills as strengths. She was direct and clear in her requests and she was unmatched when it came to driving a point home. With senior executives, she was fast on her feet and able to respond to questions fired her way. She relished these moments, where quick thinking and direct answers were called for. But people, particularly her peers, described her as impatient when others started to express their viewpoints. When it came time to facilitate a team or align multiple parties or agendas, Terri's communications repertoire fell short. While people had confidence that she could perform, she was unable to inspire others. Terri needed to learn how to better engage and motivate others around a common vision.

Those who slide to driving voice, like Terri, are often naturally skilled at advocacy. They know how to ask for what they need. But as the feedback of Terri's peers demonstrates, without the ability to listen or connect as well, advocacy will not be effective. Those who slide to supportive voice tend to have the opposite problem.

TABLE 4-1

John's and Terri's baseline and Signature Voice

	JOHN		TERRI	
	Supportive voice	**Signature Voice**	**Driving voice**	**Signature Voice**
Communication	• Openly processed thoughts out loud before making decisions • Over-used core strengths of listening and asking questions in driving for consensus	• Take a strong stand on decisions and com-municate consistently and through multiple platforms • Balance out communica-tion style to be more assertive with other partners	• Was clear, direct, and concise • Started most of her sentences with "I"	• Listen and ask more questions • Incorporate others' per-spectives in what she says

They listen and are attentive to other's needs and requests but then have a hard time taking what they hear and driving forward. John needed to add more structure to his communications so that others could easily understand where he stood, what he wanted from them and engage in productive conversations (see table 4-1).

WHY COMMUNICATION MATTERS

Communication is a fundamental leadership skill. It is the foundation for your presence. Like dribbling and shooting in basketball or throwing and hitting in baseball, communications skills are the basics that you need. There is not a leadership development program out there that doesn't in some way address how you interact and communicate with others. Communication skills are particularly important in establishing leadership presence because they are also how we connect with people. In fact, when we work with clients, we often make sure that they have the communication fundamentals down before working on other parts of their presence. This enables them to go back to those fundamentals when they feel their presence slide to one of the other quadrants.

Yet we often get lazy about communication, especially when we are crunched for time or stressed out. We take shortcuts to save time and energy. In our work, we see client after client go on autopilot when communicating. They end up getting in their own way. As with the other parts of the ACE model, executives with effective presence are intentional about the way they communicate bringing consciousness to what they say, rather than defaulting to their preferred style. They interact with others flexibly and purposefully. Strategically knowing how and when to use the core communication techniques is what can distinguish someone with exceptional presence from someone with "good-enough" presence.

Unfortunately, most people do not use all the communication techniques available to them. Instead, they return to the ones that they are most comfortable with. It's like a golfer who only uses one or two of the clubs in his bag. If he knows how to hit best with those, why would he use any others? There are two reasons for this behavior. First, as mentioned above, many people tend to go on autopilot and use the same technique over and over again. For Terri, advocating for her point of view has worked. People, especially those above her, respect her for it. So she is confounded when it doesn't work with her peers. The other reason is that individuals may want to use other techniques, but often don't know how. Terri wasn't sure she even knew what it meant to listen in a way that would drive alignment and coordination in her new role. Most people get tons of training on the technical skills of their job, but rarely does someone show them how to listen and advocate in a way that creates engaging and effective dialogue. Instead, it's expected they'll know how to do these things when they're thrust into a more senior level role.

When communicating at a leadership level, you aren't just trying to make your point, you are trying to make sure your message reaches your audience. Command and vision coupled with engagement and inspiration fill a room. To do this effectively, you must:

- Provide context and framing for your message so it is relevant for the audience

- Deliver a clear, crisp, and consistent message

- Be able to listen, engage, and connect to your audience

When you fail to meet these objectives, you miss a great opportunity to influence people with your presence and own the room. Like Terri, you may have a strong voice for self but fall short when it comes to listening. Like John, you may fail to advocate for your perspective, and slide to supportive voice. All leaders need three core communication techniques in their toolkit to support Signature Voice: *framing*, *advocacy*, and *listening and engagement*. Mastering these communication techniques will allow you to adapt in the moment and intentionally use different communication strategies to match the situation at hand and the outcome you are looking for.

FRAMING: PROVIDE CONTEXT AND VISION

Meet Juan

Juan, a newly promoted partner at a consulting firm, felt nervous going into the pitch meeting. Juan was meeting with the CEO of an energy company who was also an old friend of Bob, one of the most senior partners at Juan's firm. In fact, Bob had arranged for this business development meeting to happen. Juan had pitched the firm's work many times before, but this was a big opportunity for his practice area. The energy company was looking for a firm that could help transform its customer service organization, getting rid of unwieldy and outdated processes and refocusing the customer service representatives on what mattered most: the customer. Juan had recently completed a similar project at a credit card company and felt confident that his consulting firm was the right firm for the job but he had just gotten wind that it was up against one of its biggest competitors. Juan had practiced his pitch numerous times and thought he had the right message about why his firm and not the other was the right choice.

> *Juan:* I really appreciate the opportunity to talk to you about your customer service organization.
>
> *CEO:* We're excited you're here. You know Bob and I go way back.
>
> *Juan:* Right. I've heard that. I also heard you're looking for some help streamlining your customer service organization.
>
> *CEO:* That's right.
>
> *Juan:* We just completed a project with a major credit card company and are familiar with the issues facing large organizations trying to gain a customer focus.
>
> *CEO:* Well, we're not a credit card company. We sell energy, something everyone needs, and our customers run the gamut from wealthy to very low income.
>
> *Juan:* We've developed a methodology that identifies the key inefficiencies in customer service processes.

Juan explained the methodology, but he could see that the CEO and the other executive team members weren't fully focused. At the end of his presentation, Juan asked if they had any questions. The CEO asked, "So where do the customers fit into this?"

Juan was confused. His whole presentation had been about serving customers better. Why hadn't they gotten that?

Back at the office, Bob asked Juan how the meeting went. Juan had to admit that he wasn't sure he had engaged the team. He had covered all of his points and done the pitch just as they had rehearsed it but he wasn't sure he got through to the CEO and his team. Juan had not connected to his audience or their needs—his presence had slid to driving voice.

Why Aren't You Connecting with Your Audience?

Throughout our years of coaching and training, we've found the most difficult skill for individuals to master and yet the one with the greatest impact is *framing*. Juan had rehearsed a perfect pitch and he knew why the energy company needed his firm's services. But because he was so focused on the message he needed to deliver, he didn't frame his message so that his audience could understand it. Instead of providing the up-front context for why he was there and how his message connected to the CEO and his team, he launched into his presentation. No matter how well he delivered his pitch, the CEO was still left confused.

To drive the point home about framing, we use the following exercise in our trainings. Look at the picture of the cows below. The story about these cows is that they are sick and dying. From the picture, can you explain why that is?

PHOTO 4-1

PHOTO 4-2

Now, take a look at this second picture. Same question—why are the cows sick and dying?

Did your response change when you looked at the second picture? Were you more confident about your response? What does the second picture of the cows give you that the first doesn't? It's clear: the second picture provides context. Context is a frame that enables you to better to interpret what you see in the picture. The cows are suffering because of industrial pollution. After seeing the context, you might be more inclined to believe that the cows are dying than when you saw the picture without a frame.

Think of a picture you have in your home. Think of the frame you have put around it. What does it highlight about the picture? Does it draw your eye to a particular color or the scene in the picture? Now, imagine choosing a different frame for the picture—what would the frame draw out this time?

Framing your message has the same effect—it provides context through which others view your message and makes your message relevant to the audience. If you don't frame, there is a risk that people will provide their own using their own assumptions. After all, even a frameless picture is framed by the wall it's hanging on. Juan's audience wanted to talk about customers and the CEO even hinted at that upfront. Without explaining specifically how his pitch would help the potential client, the CEO was left wondering about what he cared most about.

Leaders need to provide similar context to align people and resources around a mission, vision, and execution to get jobs done. If they don't, people make up their own frames and stories, increasing the risk of misalignment. In 2007, Microsoft's Steve Ballmer spoke at the Stanford Business School, where he had been a student before dropping out to join Microsoft. During the Q&A portion, an audience member asked Ballmer why he had dropped out. Ballmer admitted that shortly after joining the company, he had serious doubts about his decision and was thinking of returning to business school. But then Bill Gates took him out to dinner. Ballmer recounts the experience: "At dinner, Bill said to me, 'Look, you don't get it. You may feel like you've just joined to become the bookkeeper of a thirty-person company, but we're going to put a computer on every desk and in every home.' And I swear, that recruiting pitch to keep me wound up being the mantra of the company basically for the next seventeen, eighteen years."[2] With this framing, Ballmer saw his decision to leave school, and probably every decision he made after that, in a very different context. Gates had set a vision and made it relevant to his newest employee. Gates's ability to frame the company's future in that pithy statement—"a computer on every desk and in every home"—was critical not just for Ballmer but also in inspiring others around Microsoft's mission. This is the ultimate frame a leader can provide: an inspiring vision.

FRAMING: ACTION STEPS

To effectively frame your message you first need to know your audience. Armed with the knowledge of who exactly is receiving your message and what their needs are, you can then choose an appropriate frame.

Understand Your Audience

Let's return to Juan's case. Where Juan initially went wrong was failing to understand his audience.

This begins even before the meeting when you spend time reading the backgrounds and bios of your audience and considering potential connections. Juan had a great opportunity to learn more about the CEO and what he cared about from Bob. As one tenured senior partner of a major consulting firm once shared, "You have to remember to plan for meetings so that the senior executive can unload and seek your counsel. Plan for the casual part of the interaction where you can learn about what keeps him up at night." This is especially critical when you are in an industry or role that requires you to connect and engage others quickly, where first impressions matter, such as in professional services, private equity, or customer-facing functions.

Juan got off to a rocky start because he knew he only had a short window of time and felt rushed to immediately begin with his pitch instead of with the get-to-know-yous and small talk that often precede the business talk. If Juan had asked the CEO more about the company's customers, he might have been able to frame his pitch in a way that connected more with what the CEO cared about.

Many executives find as they progress through the leadership pipeline that the number of audiences and constituencies they have to consider also increase. This requires more of their presence and their ability to convey authenticity and confidence and to connect with a variety of people. This means being intentional about considering the audience before the meeting or presentation so that the frame you choose is relevant to them: Who is the audience? What is the tone you want to strike? What outcomes do you hope to achieve from this meeting or presentation?

DRILL

Know Your Audience

Mastering the *C* in ACE gives you the adaptability to convey who you are and connect with others without sacrificing your authenticity. By equipping yourself with all the tactics and strategies available, you can handle a variety of situations and audiences.

One simple drill we offer clients is to spend a few minutes doing stakeholder analysis. Creating a frame that is relevant and will reach your audience is fundamentally tied to how they communicate, what influences them, and what keeps them up at night. If you can anchor your message to one of these issues, you are more likely to get their attention.

Try it here. Consider three key audiences or stakeholders that you interact with. Spend a few minutes deepening your understanding of them and how you might better frame your discussions with them by filling out the simple spreadsheet in table 4-2.

Clients are often surprised by how much information they glean when they stop to think about their colleagues. One client, who was at an impasse with one of his fellow executives, realized after asking this series of questions that his colleague preferred to communicate at the highest level. He only saw the big picture and moved from A to Z quickly in his thinking. As our client reflected on this, he said, "Wow! I am a linear thinker and take my time going from A to B to C when problem solving. I must be driving him crazy." He was then able to adapt his style and the framing for his messages to better suit his colleague.

Another client went through this exercise with each person on his direct report team. He has been struggling to motivate them

TABLE 4-2

Frame your discussions for stakeholders

Stakeholder or audience	Background/ history	How would you describe his/her communication style?	How is this person best influenced?	What is keeping this person up at night?
Example: Senior leader	• Originally from sales/ marketing background • Previously at x, y, z companies • Has significant international experience in global companies	• Direct • Has strong point of view • Takes initiative	• Be clear on time needed • Be direct and succinct • Focus on facts • Do not take things personally • Be able to demonstrate impact through-out global matrix	• Meeting aggressive financial targets promised to Wall Street

and keep them engaged. After considering each one as an individual, he realized he was using one communication style (his own preference) for all of them, rather than adapting it for each person. By sitting down and thinking about each of his direct reports, he better understood what their underlying motivations were and how best to communicate with them.

Choose the Right Frame

Once you have a better understanding of your audience and how they communicate, you can choose a frame that will connect with them. You have a better shot of reaching them. We are not suggesting you "spin" your message. A frame is not meant to be manipulative or to sugarcoat an unpleasant message. Instead, we're talking about frames that offer context, focus people in on the most important issues, or make your message salient to others.

There are various ways of framing a message at an executive level that exudes a confident and connected presence:

- *Strategic framing:* Tie your message to the strategic imperatives and priorities of the organization. How is what you're saying relevant to the overall business? How can you link to the bigger picture? Use the specific language of the company's goals.

- *Outcomes framing:* Connect your messages back to the goals you're trying to achieve. How is your message related to the outcomes you are trying to drive?

- *Metaphor framing:* Bring your message to life with the use of a metaphor or analogy. An executive at one of our client organizations, upon inheriting a very insular team, said to them "I need you to operate like a soccer team, not a swim team." By this, his direct reports understood that he did not want them to work in silos anymore. The metaphor made sense and had a heavier impact than him saying "I need you to work better together."

- *Sound-bites framing:* Create a pithy, memorable statement that encapsulates your overall message. If your audience forgets all the details of your message, at the very least they will still hold on to the theme. One executive repeated over and over again to his organization that the focus for the next twelve months is "relentless execution." While there were many details behind this statement, everyone understood the number-one priority.

We recently worked with Pete, a VP of Finance supporting the development function of a software entity, which was owned by a larger technology conglomerate. As part of the annual budgeting process, Pete needed to ask the CFO of the parent company for funds at a time when the parent company was tightening the reins on all budgets and going through major layoffs.

While Pete knew he had all the right slides in his presentation, he asked for our help in getting his opening frame prepared so that he could both present the case for more money while being respectful to the budgetary constraints in the rest of the organization.

Here were Pete's attempts at framing:

> *Attempt 1:* "We recognize the budgetary constraints currently at play and hate to do this, but need to ask for more money today." We agreed with Pete that this played too heavily on his voice for others and came off as apologetic.

> *Attempt 2:* "The bottom line is that we are here to ask for $500 million, given that we are the future of this company." Pete knew this didn't feel right either. It was too strongly in the driving voice quadrant: too much focus on him and his agenda, and little consideration for others.

We worked with Pete to come up with a frame that allowed his presence to be more squarely in his Signature Voice. In the end, he decided to use a strategic frame keeping both voice for self and voice for others in mind:

> *"Our intent for today is twofold: to discuss with you the investment we believe is required for our division to meet the ROI and the vision we set together to be sure our division remains a key revenue engine for the company, and to discuss how we can achieve this in the context of the budgetary constraints we are all currently under."*

This frame was not only stronger on both voice for self and voice for others, but it felt more authentic to Pete. It was a message he could get behind.

ADVOCACY: DELIVER A CLEAR, CRISP, AND CONSISTENT MESSAGE

Meet Rick

Rick is a director of quality at a large hospital in the Midwest. At a meeting with the leadership team, he was asked to update everyone on the project he was leading to reduce errors in medical records. Here is what it sounded like:

> *COO:* Rick, can you give us a sense of where your project stands?
>
> *Rick:* Sure, we've been spending the past few weeks knee-deep in the analysis, getting a sense of where the real problems lie. We've run the numbers a couple times, and I think we have some interesting findings. In a few weeks, we'll share them more broadly.
>
> *COO:* Do you think we'll get any traction with this? Are we going to need to make any large changes?
>
> *Rick:* The data seems to be supporting our original hypothesis that there are some real issues in record management. We're doing a sensitivity analysis this week.
>
> *COO:* Anything you need from me?
>
> *Rick:* I don't think so. My team is able to handle it.

The COO scratched his head. Tired of asking questions, he moved on to the next agenda item.

———————

Having a discussion with someone like Rick can be frustrating. He clearly knows a lot about the project and is keeping it on track. But it's nearly impossible to tell where he stands. He struggles to maintain his voice for self and his presence slides to supportive voice. The COO wanted a high-level update: Is the project going well or not? What could the team expect in the way of future recommendations? Instead, Rick dove into the details, explaining what the team was doing that week. Those whose presence slides into supportive voice often fall into this trap. They either don't speak up or when they do, their message is too vague or too specific to discern the salient point. Their voice for self is so weak that they don't communicate with clarity and confidence. They don't know how to advocate effectively.

Here is the feedback we got from the COO in that meeting:

> *Rick needs to enhance his communication style. He needs to learn to talk like an executive, even though he's not one yet. He needs to shift from demonstrating his value as a "doer" to showing that he is an adviser to the leadership team. He needs to stop playing the role of project manager. Instead of providing updates, he needs to give the elevator pitch: a compelling case for "Here's what we should be doing . . . " in under five minutes. I want to hear his point of view. He should be talking about things that are meaningful to the executive committee and leave the background and details for his team. When he makes the detailed comments about these smaller issues, we end up thinking of him as an in-the-weeds doer, not a thought leader.*

Why Aren't You Being Clear?

Advocacy is the ability to clearly convey your perspective. Whether you're providing feedback to a direct report, making a business case to the executive team, or communicating your vision for the future to the entire organization, you need to have a distinct point of view and communicate it in a structured way so that others know where you stand on an issue.

Leaders advocate all day long, yet so many do it poorly. When we ask senior executives how their direct reports fail to get their message across, here's what we hear:

- They are too stuck on telling me all the details and process instead of the results and the outcome.

- They know how to spot issues but they don't move to solving the problems. I want a recommendation to consider.

- They don't tell me what they need me to do to move the issue forward.

In order for Rick to shift his presence to Signature Voice and to act like a peer to the executives as the COO requested, he needed to advocate more effectively.

ADVOCACY: ACTION STEPS

To effectively advocate and increase your self-confidence and the confidence others have in you, add structure to your communications. Know your stakeholders, your stake in the ground, and the outcome you want.

Add Structure to Your Communications

People expect leaders to put a stake in the ground and push their agenda forward. You will be better equipped to communicate your message clearly and confidently by doing these three things in advance of delivering your message:

1. *Know your stakeholders:* We talked about this above. Ask yourself: What's in it for my audience? What will they want to know? What do they care about most? Think through your stakeholders' agendas, what decisions they'll have to make, and any potential issues. You want to position your message and create a frame so that it is relevant to them.

2. *Know your stake in the ground:* Be clear on what the message is. What is it you want to say? Are you sharing difficult news? Are you making a request? Figure out what the takeaway is. Once you know your main point

and what you want your audience to do about it, you can decide what details are necessary. Always communicate the "bottom line up front" and then support your statement with data and explanation. If you have three points to make, then make your enumeration explicit up front. Putting your thoughts into buckets or categories up front can help your audience track what you are saying (see "John Puts a Firmer Stake in the Ground").

3. *Know what outcome you want:* Last, you need to think about what you want to happen when you're done communicating. Do you want the audience to give you the green light to move forward? Do you need them to give you more resources? Figure out how you can enroll your audience in the outcome and get them on board.

If Rick had advocated effectively, here is how the conversation could have gone:

COO: Rick, can you give us a sense of where your project stands?

Rick: Sure. To ensure we get the most from the proposed change [*this is the strategic frame*], we've surfaced two critical findings that have an impact on medical records as well as strategic implications for the hospital [*this is the key message*]: one [*here comes the structure*], we have a tremendous opportunity to improve turnaround time through the use of better technologies; two, we can significantly minimize our overall risk exposure by eliminating some of the steps in information transfer. At this point, we are further analyzing and quantifying the results and should be prepared to share the whole report in a few weeks. One request [*here he's ensuring the outcome*] would be to get your perspective on which people from the executive team I should brief prior to the full report out. I have some ideas, but it would be good to run those by you offline.

COO: Sounds good. I'll give it some thought, and let's plan to discuss later this week.

Structured advocacy is one of the key skills high-potential managers must master, and it goes a long way in building a more confident presence. The skill can be used across all mediums: delivering

JOHN PUTS A FIRMER STAKE IN THE GROUND

When firm issues arose that needed resolution, John often went to other partners first to ask their opinion of the situation. One of the partners shared, "It feels like he's constantly throwing a ball over the wall, expecting others to solve the problem rather than stepping up to the plate and offering a perspective first."

When we asked John about this, he said that he had always been successful working with CEO clients by acting the role of trusted adviser—he asked them insightful questions and used a collaborative discovery process to arrive at an answer. This worked so well with clients because they were bought into the solution by the time they reached an answer. But what John didn't realize is this same approach wasn't working with his fellow partners. What appeared insightful and skilled to clients outside his organization came off as weak and indecisive inside the organization with his peers. We worked with him to adjust his approach and reverse the order of his conversations when discussing problems or issues with peers:

1. Start by sharing a thoughtful point of view on how to respond to the situation (lead with voice for self).

2. Then maintain his natural openness by asking for others' thoughts and reactions to his proposal (maintain, but don't lead with, voice for others).

This subtle shift in his communication strategy greatly enhanced his presence. John appeared more proactive than reactive with the other partners.

PowerPoint presentations, drafting e-mails, engaging in in-person discussions, presenting at meetings, leaving voice mails, and even interacting informally with colleagues.

Structured advocacy takes some preparation and practice. It can be helpful to distill thoughts into bullet points before you speak so you are inclined to keep your presentation punchy and concise. Some leaders have learned over time to create preparation rituals that help them to move their presentations from unorganized, stream-of-consciousness thoughts to the succinct, pithy, seemingly extemporaneous deliveries that leave others in awe. Winston Churchill was known for writing out his speeches, tearing them up, writing them again, tearing them up again, and writing them again, so that by time he delivered a speech, the words were his own, in his head, and the delivery sounded unrehearsed rather than canned.

LISTENING AND ENGAGING: INCREASE CONNECTION AND INSPIRATION

Meet Susan

Susan is a vice president of communications in an entertainment company with a strong reputation for moving at a fast pace, responding to tight deadlines, and keeping her team focused and working hard. Unfortunately, she is also known for burning through team members. They learn a lot from her and then choose to move elsewhere in the company, usually to lower their stress and find better balance. When we shadowed her at one of her team meetings, this is what we heard:

> *Susan:* All right, what do we have on deck for today? Darren, can you update us on the website launch?

> *Darren:* Sure. The designers have proposed various templates for us to look at . . .

> *Susan:* What templates? I haven't seen them yet.

Darren: We just received them yesterday, and I wanted to vet them before getting everyone's input. At first look, they look pretty good.

Susan: Well, as long as they're good. Do they reflect the new brand? That's our top priority for this launch. Marketing has been clear about this: we need to be sure everything is aligned with the new brand, whether online or not. If not, it's not worth our time.

Darren: Yes, I think it's aligned, but quite honestly, I need to take a closer look. I wanted to do that and then I planned to circulate . . .

Susan: Don't take too long doing that. Time is ticking, and we've got to move this along. Rachel, where are we with the press release?

Darren sat back in his chair. He looked flustered and defeated.

Why Aren't You Listening?

We have all been in meetings where, like Darren, we don't feel heard. It doesn't feel good; you aren't engaged or connected to the other person. And at the end of the day, it is difficult to trust that the person cares about what you have to say. Susan framed her message and delivered a clear message but she didn't realize the impact she had on Darren. She moved on to the next topic because that was what she was comfortable doing: moving through agenda items quickly and efficiently. But having effective leadership presence requires that you not only provide vision and a clear message but that you make a connection with others as well. Otherwise, people assume you are just a talking head. Listening is one of the key communication techniques to drive that. Susan's boss, the SVP of Public Relations, had this to say:

Susan needs to work on listening. She needs to hear what folks are saying and make it obvious that she is taking it in and digesting it. Susan can come across as defensive when challenged, and as a result others don't feel heard. She doesn't seem to read or listen to the emotional cues the audience is giving her when they are upset or frustrated. It's clear in their body language, but she just continues talking. Sometimes she focuses too much on the deliverable at the expense of what is right for the situation or her relationships with others. She can maintain her powerful communication style—it's an asset for sure—but she needs to be less forceful. She needs to ask more questions and explicitly show others that she cares about what they have to say. She needs to listen more.

While "Listen more" is a simple message, it is not as easy as one might think. Many of our clients whose presence slides to driving voice don't feel they need to listen. They can rationalize (almost convincingly) why they don't do it:

- I already know the answer.

- It's a waste of time.

- I am distracted by everything else on my plate.

- I am focused on getting my point across and getting my way.

- I honestly don't care how the other person sees the situation.

- I am doing most of the talking.

What these leaders fail to realize is that by not listening, they are taking a big risk. Influencing people is far more effective than pushing them in a certain direction and to influence, you need an awareness of others' viewpoints. We discussed in the chapter 3 how dangerous failure to see others' perspectives can be. If you are caught up in your own stuff and not aware of the other perspective, you are missing an important opportunity to influence. Listening isn't just important in one-on-one conversations or team meetings. At the most senior levels, an executive's ability to listen to what is going on inside and outside of the organization is critical to having Signature Voice. You must sense what people are thinking and feeling without being directly told. You need to interpret what's being said in employee engagement surveys, the underlying message in customer complaints, and even the mood in the company cafeteria. This kind of listening is the prerequisite to setting a vision and mobilizing an organization to fulfill it.

Take Robin, a senior leader who had transitioned from leading technology transformation at a prominent brokerage firm to a chief technology officer role in a regional credit union bank. He was hired by the regional bank specifically for his ability to lead large-scale IT transformations. However, after only a few months, others began to feel that the way he communicated changes wasn't working. This is what we heard from one of his team members: "While Robin has the right intention, he talks to us like we're on Wall Street. This isn't Wall Street. It's Ohio. And here you have to listen, engage others in the process, and motivate them based on the mission. We care less about the financial reward than he seems to think, and he keeps alienating us by leading with it every time he talks. If he would only take the time to listen, it would go a long way." Clearly, Robin's communication strategies, which likely worked well in his previous role, were sabotaging his presence in this new situation and putting his success as risk. For his part, Robin was increasingly frustrated. For all the all-hands and skip-level meetings he was conducting, he couldn't understand why he wasn't getting through to his team and others at the bank. Robin had lost touch with his voice for others in the context of the new organizational culture, and his presence slid to driving voice.

In order for Susan, Robin, and others like them to begin listening more effectively, they have to realize that listening isn't about being nice (though there's nothing wrong with being kind, of course). Listening is a skill that enables you to align people, decisions, and agendas. You cannot have leadership presence without hearing what others are saying.

LISTENING AND ENGAGING: ACTION STEPS

To improve your ability to listen and engage, you need to master three levels of listening—surface, issues-based, and emotions-based. Digging deeper into what you hear requires you learn to ask insightful questions.

Master the Three Levels of Listening

Listening isn't just about hearing the words people say in a dialogue or group conversation. You need to be listening both in the meeting room and outside it. People reveal important information, motivations, and cues during any interaction, and you need to be listening at all moments, constantly reading the room. Through years of working with executives in coaching and training, we've identified three levels at which you need to be attentive to other people's words and actions in order to have effective presence:

- Surface listening

- Issues-based listening

- Emotions-based listening

LEVEL 1: SURFACE LISTENING. Surface listening is something you learn to do at a young age when you pay attention in school and hear what your teachers or parents are saying. Chances are you've mastered this first level. This is when you listen to what's actually being said and take the words at face value. You demonstrate that you are focused by making eye contact, nodding your head, and repeating back what you heard (often called reflective listening). This is an initial move toward establishing a connection with your audience.

Surface listening will only get you so far. Unfortunately, many leaders whose presence slides to driving voice stop here. They mistake listening as agreeing with another person's perspective. *But there is a fundamental difference between recognizing that you heard the message and signaling that you agree with it.* Hearing what is being said is like signing for a FedEx package. You've consented to take a look inside. You haven't guaranteed that you are going to like it or keep it. Instead, you're maintaining an openness and seeing if it influences your thinking. In order to strengthen your voice for others, you must take your listening to the next two levels: issues-based listening and emotion-based listening.

LEVEL 2: ISSUES-BASED LISTENING. Issues-based listening is the ability to cut through the clutter of what's being said and focus on what matters. Rather than listening to just the basic facts, you are on the lookout for the underlying message. You ask yourself: *What are the implications of what's being said? What are the key issues at hand?* Sometimes this requires asking questions. Open-ended inquiries help you uncover the underlying meaning. You can ask: *What do you mean by that? Why do you think that is? What do others think?* By getting the person to talk more, you'll learn what isn't immediately obvious. We talk more about asking insightful questions below.

LEVEL 3: EMOTIONS-BASED LISTENING. Emotion-based listening is the deepest level and with it, you can uncover the true agenda at play. Leaders who listen at this level sense the underlying emotion and motivation behind the issues. They are able to understand what is keeping the other person up at night. They listen not just to the words but also the nonverbal cues, such as the stakeholder's body language, tone of voice, and overall mood. They get to the root of the issues by revealing the assumptions the stakeholder has made. Here's where true acknowledgment happens. Once you understand what's going on underneath the surface, you then name it and acknowledge it. You can say something like, "It sounds like our team's reaction to your report has upset you" or "I hear you saying that what you care about most is completing the project on time and within budget." Having done that, you can then move

TERRI PRACTICES THREE LEVELS OF LISTENING

Terri admitted to us that there were times when she wasn't that interested in what others had to say. She wasn't surprised to be accused of "going deaf" because there were times she wasn't listening at all: instead, she was thinking about the next meeting she was going to or how she would report to the senior team what the group had just decided. Terri needed to practice all three levels of listening and made a concerted effort. But she found that the heightened consciousness about needing to pay attention left her more agitated and impatient in meetings. It was too much pressure, and after a few weeks, she told us she didn't think it was working at all.

So we had Terri start in a different setting: at home. We encouraged her to try the three levels of listening with her two sons. We asked her to ask the boys about something they cared about. Terri said that was easy: their hockey game. Terri then practiced each level of listening, first listening to what they said about the upcoming game, nodding and reflecting back what she heard. Terri said this was awkward at first, but the boys got more animated the more they sensed she was being attentive. Terri then tried out asking open-ended questions. What did their coach feel about the game? What kinds of things were they worried about? Terri said the end result was that she felt more connected to her sons. She better understood the breadth of emotions they had about their upcoming game and felt more equipped to help them prepare for it.

Once she'd practiced at home, we asked her to try to do the same thing at work. Terri was tempted to give in to her default instincts—jumping in when others weren't giving her the answer she wanted to hear, or failing to ask questions—but she could get through these moments by remembering how well it worked with her boys. Ultimately, Terri's skill conditioning required rewiring years of habit through intentional practice.

into the conversation. Often times, the other party just needs acknowledgment of the core motivation, hot button, or emotion before they can receive your message or engage in a true dialogue.

Emotions-based listening requires you to be objective, open and curious. It takes focus and effort to be this present. While it's a critical leadership skill to be able to do that when necessary, it's not essential at all times. The key is to be able to practice all three levels of listening and then strategically decide which level is required for each situation (see "Terri Practices Three Levels of Listening").

Ask Insightful Questions

Listening is not a one-way street. While you are taking in information, you are also making a connection and ensuring your audience knows you're following them. To shrink the table between you and the person (or people) you are interacting with you, you need to be able to ask insightful questions. With such questions, you portray a depth of understanding and business acumen without having to declare it outright. Great questions keep the flow of the discussion going, show your interest in the other party's agenda, and form a bridge between you and your audience. We often tell clients that, when in doubt in a meeting or conversation, ask a great question. The result is that your audience leaves the interaction feeling you genuinely understood their issues.

You can use these questions in a strategic manner to focus your audience on what matters, the common goal, or shared interests. The objective is not to put anyone on the witness stand but to elicit a rich, productive discussion by drawing out insights you might not have thought of.

Some sample questions include:

- What outcomes do you hope to achieve with this work?

- If you could only focus on three priorities, which ones do you think would move the needle the most?

- Can you tell me more about your thinking behind that?

- What have customers or others shared with you about that issue?

- What conditions would need to be in place for that option to be viable?

- What ideas or resources have you tried to drive the necessary changes? What worked well? What didn't?

Each of these questions elicits continued elaboration and discussion. They encourage your counterpart to stop and think, engage with the topic, and feel like part of the problem-solving process. Typically, a good rule of thumb is that questions that start with open-ended phrases like "What . . . ?" "How . . . ?" or "Can you tell me more?" invite further discussion better than ones that begin with phrases like "Do you think . . . ?" Such closed-ended questions invite simple yes or no answers and often shut down a conversation.

One of our clients found this especially useful when he was presenting to the executive team and got pushback on his ideas. Rather than yielding (and giving up his voice for self) or pushing back and restating his opinion defensively (and losing sight of his voice for others), he would ask an insightful question to keep his idea alive. Just one shrewd question usually led to healthy, productive debate. He found that the end result—whatever he and the other executive team members landed on—was better than where he had started.

BEYOND LISTENING AND ASKING QUESTIONS: STRATEGIES FOR INCREASING ENGAGEMENT

Listening and asking questions is just the starting point. Table 4-3 shows a list of other strategies we've helped leaders add to their repertoires in order to connect with others. In settings with large

TABLE 4-3

Strategies for increasing engagement

Communication strategy	What it is	Benefit
Icebreakers/rapport builders	• Conversation pieces for unplanned, informal parts of a meeting prior to the start, during breaks, or in the hallway	• Puts others at ease • Helps everyone warm up • Builds rapport and sets the right tone
Bridging	• Use of words, language, or phrases to make a link between you and other person/audience	• Connects leader to audience
Acknowledging	• Verbal recognition of a job well done • Authentically giving credit, celebrating a significant milestone	• Increases engagement and motivates others
Storytelling	• Relevant anecdotes of key experiences or memories that drive a point home	• Helps people identify with you • Gives meaning to your messages
Sound bites	• Key messages made memorable for audience in pithy phrases	• Cuts through the noise

audiences, such as town halls or companywide meetings, where it's difficult to connect with each individual, leaders still need to find ways to engage with the audience as if they were in a one-on-one conversation. Adding appropriate, relevant stories or acknowledging what the team has accomplished can go a long way to helping a leader appear in touch, even when he has multiple layers of staff within his sphere of influence.

SKILL CONDITIONING: BRINGING IT ALL TOGETHER

In real business situations, you aren't ever just framing, advocating, or listening. In fact, *you need to do all three adaptively and flexibly often in the course of one conversation.* For example, executives who are especially adept at framing don't just use it at the start of a meeting or discussion but know how to fluidly and adaptively reframe their points during a conversation to maintain a connection with the audience. This is a true distinction between those with good leadership presence and those whose presence is in Signature Voice: they use all of the communication skills available to them.

None of these skills can be a one-way street: you can't be purely hearing what someone else is saying or stating your viewpoint. You are in Signature Voice when you are in an active dialogue, engaged with another person or audience. This is when communication moves from a one-way dialogue to a two-way street, and you can easily oscillate between your voice for self and your voice for others. Leaders with the full communication repertoire can respond to any ball that is thrown their way—they are able to present their views, answer questions thrown their way, and engage and get the other person talking.

`DRILL`

Executive Meeting

Presenting at an executive meeting is an opportunity to prove your mettle as a leader and gain the support of the most senior people in your organization. As such, it is a situation in which it is critical to have Signature Voice presence. This meeting, more than almost any other situation, requires leaders to adaptively and fluidly demonstrate a clear, consistent, confident voice for self while maintaining a voice for others to influence those in the room. You usually have limited time, and your audience usually has limited patience.

When presenting to a roomful of executives, you must frame your message so that it is relevant to the group's priorities and vision, advocate your message in a clear, concise, and structured way; and listen, engage, and connect with the group to encourage a fruitful discussion. And you need to do this all while watching the clock. It's a true challenge; the best leaders spend lots of time preparing for it.

Consider an upcoming update or meeting you have with your function or organization's executive team. How can you use the *C* in ACE to help you prepare?

1. Who is the audience? What tone do you want to strike? What outcomes do you want to achieve?

2. What frame and organizing structure will you use?

3. What are the key points you need to make?

4. What are some strategic questions you can keep in your back pocket to engage the audience if necessary?

5. How will you listen and look for cues to engage and connect to your audience?

This kind of preparation is critical for formal meetings but it can be just as useful for those spontaneous conversations in the hallway or during in a cab ride with an executive peer or leader who asks you "How's it going?" For these situations, it's useful to think through how you will respond. Prepare a succinct framing headline and three bullet points to have in your back pocket.

WHAT TO REMEMBER

- Communication strategies are an important part of conditioning for Signature Voice. Here is where you can gain the most traction for building your leadership presence because the way you communicate is what people experience most clearly when they interact with you: the words coming out of your mouth.

- Leaders with Signature Voice have a full communications repertoire and utilize different communication strategies, depending on the audience and the situation.

- Framing your message provides your audience with the context to interpret your message. Frames focus people on the most important issues and make your message salient to others. There are several types of frames, including strategic frames, outcomes frames, metaphor frames, and sound-bites frames. The ultimate frame a leader can provide is a vision of the future.

- You can strengthen your voice for self by building your ability to advocate. Structured advocacy requires knowing your audience, your stake in the ground, and identifying the outcome you want to achieve. Structure your speech by organizing points into buckets and categories.

- Even with a great frame and clear message, you have to be able to connect and engage your audience. You can increase your voice for others by conditioning your listening skills. There are three levels of listening that a leader can use strategically, depending on the situation and the audience: surface listening, issues-based listening, and the deepest level, emotions-based listening. Asking insightful questions keeps the conversation flowing, demonstrates your interest in the issues, and forges a connection with your audience. Other connector strategies can also help you engage and in-fluence your audience in small forums, such as one-on-one discussions or in larger settings, such as all-hands meetings or skip-levels.

CHAPTER FIVE

ENERGY
Physical Conditioning

I n chapter 4, we talked about influencing and connecting with people through what you say. The final lever you pull to condition for Signature Voice is the *E* in ACE: *energy*. People interpret you as a leader through your physical presence and energy. Based on what your body language says and your image projects, they make assumptions about what you are thinking and feeling, regardless of what you are saying. Far too often, executives fail to align their physical energy with what they want to achieve. When we talk about energy, we mean both the superficial layer— how you look—and the vibe you give off—the mood and tone you convey. How you appear to others matters as much as what you say.

Throughout coaching, John struggled with the feedback that he appeared physically exhausted. The partners said he looked on the brink of burnout. One said that John always looked frazzled and increasingly "not put together." Many also noted how he was repeatedly late to meetings and slow to respond to e-mails and calls. The partners knew he was highly committed and often burned the midnight oil but they wondered at what cost. The appearance of not being in control eroded the partners' confidence in him. They were also concerned about what would happen if he took on the broader responsibilities required of the North America managing partner. Although John was committed to finding his Signature Voice, he was both frustrated by this feedback and humbled by it. On the one hand, if all the partners cared about was his style, not his substance and how hard he was working, he wasn't sure he'd be able to meet their expectations. On the other hand, he admitted how tired he felt and that he'd gained quite a bit of weight over the past few years. "Honestly, I'm actually concerned about how sustainable my pace is in terms of my health. But I have a hard time seeing how to get all the work done without sacrificing something," he said.

Terri also had trouble with how her energy was perceived. She knew that people appreciated her ability to drive a point home, so why were they so worked up about those times when she did it? Her peers described her energy as occasionally "overbearing." Her voice got louder when people asked questions, and when really pressed on a point, she occasionally rolled her eyes. One direct report talked about how Terri had a habit of pointing her finger whenever she spoke to him in a meeting—as if she were making an accusation. Terri listened to this feedback but questioned how useful it was. She wasn't going to back down when she believed in something. Besides, was this about protecting other people's feelings? If they were thicker-skinned, none of this would matter.

These were critical areas that both John and Terri needed to focus on to reach Signature Voice (see table 5-1).

Most people find it hard to comprehend how they are being perceived physically. Without a mirror angled at you at all times, you truly don't understand what others are seeing. In many of our trainings and coaching sessions, we use a video camera to help clients see what their *E* in ACE looks like. We play back the video and talk with them about what they perceive and what others likely perceive as well. Many say this has both dispelled concerns about how they physically appeared to others or increased

TABLE 5-1

John's and Terri's baseline and Signature Voice energy

| | JOHN | | TERRI | |
	Supportive voice	Signature Voice	Driving voice	Signature Voice
Energy	• Appeared weary • Appeared flustered • Was not visible enough to broader partner group	• Invest in physical self-care • Put structures in place to help prioritize and manage schedule and capacity • Identify ways to engage a broader set of partners	• Came off as strong and overbearing • Was easily annoyed and curt • Sounded like she was always judging	• Convey composure when required • Give less judgmental nonverbal cues

their awareness of things of which they hadn't previously been conscious.

WHY ENERGY MATTERS

Many communication studies find that somewhere between 70 and 95 percent of what's "heard" during a conversation is through nonverbal cues.[1] Whether you intend to or not, you send strong messages to people through your body language and energy. By looking at you, they make assessments about your knowledge, expertise, and competence as a leader. Many leaders, knowing this, focus almost exclusively on their physicality to improve their presence. They hope for a silver bullet that will automatically make them appear more like leaders and they model themselves on a common image: someone who dresses well or stands taller. Sharpening up your "book cover" certainly yields positive

YOU AREN'T JUST JUDGED BY YOUR BOOK COVER

It's impossible to talk about executive presence without addressing the "book cover" of a leader: the most outer, visible layer of presence that creates a first impression. This is how you dress, how you style your hair, etc. Many leaders ask the question: *Should I conform to the dress code of my organization even if it's not my style, or can I use dress as a form of self-expression?* Most people have an opinion on this, but few people talk about it. It's a sensitive subject. In fact, we've spoken with many senior leaders who say this is one of the single toughest pieces of feedback to give someone, especially if it's getting in the way of their success. Who wants to tell someone that his ill-fitting suits are contributing to his inability to get promoted?

The good news is that this isn't a major issue for most people. The issue of a leader's book cover has come up in less than 20 percent of our coaching engagements. That said, it's important to talk about how a leader can address this issue and what his manager can do to help.

First, here are some of the things we hear about this issue:

- "He's an officer now. He needs to upgrade his wardrobe to fit the role."

- "Now that she's representing the organization externally, she needs to sharpen up her 'presentation' in terms of style and dress."

- "I was happy to see he was looking more crisp, put together, and polished than before."

When clients struggle with their book cover, we often encourage them to work with a professional stylist to help them achieve a look that is congruent with the presence they want. Some of our clients will engage with independent stylists and others will work with personal shoppers, who are often offered as a complimentary service by department stores and boutiques. Regardless of whom they choose to work with, the stylists tend to reinforce certain tips:

- Tailored clothing that fits appropriately can help increase your overall presence.

- Groomed hair also goes a long way.

- For women, coordinated accessories and subtle makeup are nuanced ways to improve others' perceptions of you.

Voice for self and voice for others are just as relevant here. In this case, building a voice for others is acknowledging and adhering to your organization's, and even industry's, norms around dress. Enhancing your voice for self here is about finding a style that is authentic and comfortable for you. We had one client, an up-and-coming star in a financial services firm where suits were the norm. After we had shared with him a mountain of feedback about his presence, he explained that he had selected his suit brand because "that was what all the partners wore." The problem was, he wasn't comfortable in these suits and it showed. People perceived him as hesitant and awkward. We talked at length with him about what would feel like a more authentic style, and he ended up switching to a different brand, which fit him much better. This, of course, wasn't the complete answer to his presence issues, but it was the first step toward being more comfortable in his own skin, which is exactly what we aim for in the *E* in ACE.

Style is not a cure-all, but it is important and must be married with substance and authenticity.

---

benefits (see "You Aren't Just Judged by Your Book Cover"), but it won't help you fully realize the impact you want to have as a leader. You need to address the full spectrum of physical elements that drive presence.

The energy you give off has incredible impact beyond how good you look or how crisp your presentation is. Instead of acting out or copying what you think success looks like, physically condition yourself to find an authentic energy that connects with others. There's something incredibly appealing and magnetic about someone who is truly at ease, relaxed, and comfortable in her own skin.

BODY LANGUAGE: MANAGE
WHAT YOUR BODY SAYS

Meet Patricia

As a senior director of new product development in a fast-moving consumer goods company, Patricia played a critical role in determining which products move from product development to the prelaunch phase. At a meeting to decide the fate of one product, she felt her shoulders tense, and she started to shift in her chair. She was annoyed that her colleagues were rehashing a point that she thought they had resolved last week. *Why can't they be more efficient?* she wondered. As she interrupted the conversation to make her point, she started to speak faster and raise her voice. In response, she noticed her colleagues look down at the table. Some swiveled their chairs away. She knew she was losing them, but wasn't sure how to get them back. Leaning forward on the table, she asked what they thought, but didn't get much of a response.

What Is Your Body Telling You and Others?

This was not an uncommon place for Patricia to end up in. Her presence sometimes slid to driving voice, as it did at this moment. Over the years, she had gotten feedback that maintaining her composure was a key development area. She had a reputation for being assertive with her body language and raising her voice when she was not happy with the way a meeting was going or with what one of her direct reports was saying. These actions signaled to those in the room that she was not interested in a two-way dialogue. Patricia had been told that she needed to listen better. What she didn't realize the first time she heard that feedback was that she couldn't just listen with her mind, but she had to demonstrate openness with her body. She had essentially lost her audience, not because of anything she had said but because of the energy she gave off through her nonverbal cues.

When we worked with Patricia in coaching, we focused on developing an awareness of the message her body language sends. We helped her see that when she raised her voice and started talking faster, she was shutting people out of the conversation, telling them that she would take control from here on out. This isn't what Patricia wanted. In fact, she found herself frustrated with her team, that they held back and didn't assert themselves more. By sharing feedback from the team, we helped her see that while the team could be more assertive, she was causing much of their reticence. They expressed the desire to speak up but explained that they were hesitant to do so. For some, it was about fear, and for others, it was pure annoyance.

This meeting was tough for Patricia. In retrospect, she could see that her colleagues had pushed one of her hot buttons. They challenged her values of efficiency and decisiveness and she was beginning to lose her composure. We worked with her to calm herself down before she fell down that familiar rabbit hole. Patricia developed tactics for when she began to see signs of getting hijacked by her emotions and headed toward a heated discussion. Instead of raising her voice and further driving home her points, she learned to take a deep breath and steady herself by anchoring her foot into the floor. When she did that, she was able to remain engaged with her team, maintain her composure, and prevent her slide to driving voice. Her self-control then allowed for others in the room to contribute to the discussion.

Working with the body and energy is often a foreign concept for leaders. Some hear the word *energy* and ask, "Is this new age?" or say "I don't want anything too woo-woo." The starting point for these individuals is to build some awareness around their physical selves and what their bodies communicate to others. Again, videotaping or getting feedback from important stakeholders can be helpful here. With the awareness these techniques build, many leaders see potential in two areas where they hadn't before. One, they are able to build physical endurance needed for the demands of their jobs. And two, they can better manage the "wake" of their presence.

BODY LANGUAGE: ACTION STEPS

To maintain control over what your body language communicates, you need to identify and manage the physical cues you send to others and restore your energy so you have the physical endurance you need as a leader.

Identify the Physical Cues

In today's 24/7 world, we spend much of our time in our own heads. For many individuals, focusing on their bodies can be a new and uncomfortable experience. The idea of body language may seem amorphous. We created the framework shown in table 5-2 to help make the concepts more tangible. It lists six cue points where individuals signal to others what they are thinking and feeling. When your presence slides out of Signature Voice into one of the other quadrants, you communicate that through these unconscious signals.

We use the acronym CENTER to help leaders remember each of these cue points. As you slide out of Signature Voice you become "uncentered." Patricia watched out for times when she felt off-center and used the six cue points to help her return to her Signature Voice. She did this in two ways. First, she increased her own awareness of what she experienced in each of the six areas when she began to slip. She was lucky to have zeroed in on the physical attribute that caused her to most often lose her

TABLE 5-2

CENTER: Six body language cues

	What others may see when you slide to supportive voice	What others may see when you slide to driving voice
Core posture	• Slouched, loose posture	• Rigid, tense, wound-up posture
Eye contact	• Not holding eye contact	• Intense eye contact
Natural gestures	• Nervous gestures, fidgeting	• Aggressive gestures like finger pointing
Tone, tempo, timing	• High pitch or soft volume • Use of filler words such as "um" or "ah"; stutters	• Fast pace or loud volume • Judgmental or condescending tone
Expressions of the face	• Deer-in-headlights wide eyes	• Furrowed brows
Regions and Territory	• Shrinks down, does not take up enough space or fill the room	• Takes up too much space at the table or in the room
Overall impression	• Apologetic stance • Not comfortable in one's own skin • Overly defensive	• Overbearing stance • Arrogant • Annoyed • Judgmental

audience—the tone and tempo of her voice. When her voice got louder and her speech picked up speed, she gave the impression that she was judging or condescending to those in the room. When she sounded critical and came off as a scolding parent, her message and expertise became irrelevant. She learned to watch out for her shoulders tensing, her voice getting louder. When she felt the urge to lean into a table, taking up more room, she knew she was headed into a slide into driving voice. These were the clues that she needed to slow down and take a deep breath. Second, she also let her team know she was working on this and gave them permission to offer feedback on her nonverbal cues.

By being aware of each of the points, you can take an inventory of how your presence is being perceived. The key is to catch the presence slide before it jeopardizes the situation. To do this, look for clues that the slide is beginning to happen. John noticed that when he was meeting with another partner and a potential conflict arose, he would begin to slouch slightly. He knew this wasn't visible to his counterpart, but he could feel his shoulders bend forward slightly and he would play with his pen. These subtle cues helped remind John to bring his attention back to his perspective and focus on the strategic purpose of the meeting and what he wanted to achieve rather than what his peer partner might be thinking.

Unfortunately, negative interactions create stronger impressions than positive ones. Some studies say that the negative ones have fives times larger impact than pleasant ones.[2] Therefore, unpleasant interactions can have a negating effect whereby people don't remember or value all of the other agreeable interactions you've had. One of Terri's peers told us that in reality probably only three out of ten of their exchanges were disagreeable, but that when he thought of Terri, he was left with the impression that she thought she was better than him. In their article "What Creates Energy in Organizations?" Rob Cross, Wayne Baker, and Andrew Parker talk about the impact that people like Terri can have on those around them. They describe people who "have an uncanny ability to drain the life out of a group. These energy-sappers are avoided whenever possible, even when they have an expertise to contribute to solving a problem."[3] This is why it's critical to manage your physical cues.

It is difficult to pick up on your own physical cues. One of our clients, Joe, was shocked by feedback he received from his colleagues. This is what people told us about him:

- "Whenever I—or someone else—talks, he makes this face where he scrunches up all his features. It makes me feel like he thinks I'm wrong."

- "Sometimes his facial expressions are hard to read—does he not agree with what I am saying?"

Joe was disappointed. He had never intended to make others feel like he didn't care or was disengaged. He simply thought he was doing his job, and doing it well, but his presence slid to driving voice, and his body language was betraying him as a result. We recorded Joe in a discussion with a colleague so that he could see what was happening. A light bulb switched on when Joe watched the video. He couldn't believe it: what others perceived as condescension or disagreement was actually his way of processing information. He saw the faces he made and understood why others had misunderstood. Joe was able to better manage his expressions but he also talked with key colleagues to explain that he was aware of the perception he was giving, but that was not his intention. His coworkers appreciated his candor and were able to better interpret his body language.

DRILL

Build Awareness of Your First Impressions

Because first impressions are hard to erase, we encourage leaders to develop a keen awareness of their book cover and nonverbal CENTER cues. This is a starting point to altering the impression you make.

Answer the following questions about yourself, quickly. Don't take longer than a minute on each one. Be as specific and honest as possible. Don't think too hard about it. Just write down what comes to mind.

What adjectives would you use to describe the first impression you make on others?

_____

_____

_____

(continued)

What assumptions might others make based on your physical presence? (Think about book cover and the six cue points of CENTER.)

_____

_____

_____

To get the most out of this drill, it's best to ask a colleague to answer the same questions on your behalf. When he gives you his feedback, ask follow-up questions such as, "What do I do specifically that gives you that impression?" or simply thank him for his time and honesty. With feedback in hand, you now have the power to assess whether the impression you give is what you intend. Is there congruence between your self-assessment and your colleague's feedback or is there a gap? View any gaps as opportunities to improve your physical presence.

Restore Your Energy

Once you are more aware of your body and the energy you give off, the next step is to condition the executive endurance needed for the role you are in. In today's corporate environment, stress and pressure are givens. In a study conducted by the Center for Creative Leadership, 80 percent of leaders reported that work was the primary source of stress in their lives. Being in a leadership role increases that level of stress.[4] Learning how to physically condition your presence while making sure you feel your physical best is critical to maintaining a positive impact on your teams and organization.

The reality is, energy is not an endless resource. It needs to be continually replenished and restored. One of our favorite books about energy management is Tony Schwartz and Jim Loehr's *The Power of Full Engagement*. Schwartz and Loehr describe the importance of energy this way: "Energy is simply the capacity to do work. Our most fundamental need as human beings is to spend and recover energy . . . Leaders and managers make a fundamental mistake when they assume that they can overlook the physical dimension of energy and still expect those who work for them to perform at their best."[5]

This means becoming aware of which physical levers set you up to be at your personal best. For some this requires careful observation over a set period of time, paying attention to the meetings and interactions that went particularly well. After such a meeting, jot down your physical condition. Over the years, we've heard responses such as:

- "The key for me is getting a good night's sleep."

- "I realize when I hold off on the coffee the morning of a big presentation I am much more calm."

- "Getting exercise is absolutely critical for me."

- "Staying off sugar has helped me to keep my mood in check."

The answer to maintaining energy is individual to each person. Generally, we've found that for leaders whose presence tends to slide to driving voice, calming and focusing activities help increase voice for others. For those who slid more often to supporting voice, we found that activities that build strength help them tap into the voice for self (for example, see "How Did John Restore His Energy"?). One of our clients who often slid to supporting voice transformed his physical confidence by taking up a new Ashtanga yoga practice.

Once you find an activity that works for you, use it in a strategic way to bolster your presence when it's needed more: take a spin class the night before a big presentation, take five minutes to meditate and breathe during a long day of meetings. Patricia discovered that if she went running on mornings she had scheduled meetings with her team, she was calmer and more focused during the day, less apt to be triggered. Terri found the same thing about running—it relaxed her and released tension, which then helped her to be more patient.

HOW DID JOHN RESTORE HIS ENERGY?

John had a breakthrough in his coaching when he realized that the senior partners were not asking him to put style over substance. Instead, he needed to find his own authentic way to show up as a confident and energizing leader—and this was something he needed to do for himself, not for others. Since he was working on increasing his voice for self, this was a great place to start. We reminded him that he needed to do this while maintaining his strong voice for others. He took steps to care for himself physically and feed the energy he so badly needed. He returned to the basics: he restarted a workout regimen and hired a personal trainer to help him stick to it. He engaged his executive assistant to help him better manage his calendar—one of the most helpful things they did was block times on his calendar where he could focus on the high-priority work. This all made him appear less frazzled and more in control of his schedule and his time. He exuded increased confidence and several of his fellow partners took notice.

Patricia stayed committed to her running because she relished the moments when she felt she was at her personal best as a leader. She described these times as being "in the zone." She felt energized and capable of motivating others. This was in stark contrast to feeling drained and bringing others down. When we asked her what her energy felt like during those positive times, she said she felt:

- Strong and approachable

- Polished and humble

- Authentic and connected

- Able to hold the hard line with someone while also treating the person with dignity and respect

Remembering these moments motivated her to continually improve her presence, and she set a goal to increase the amount of time she felt this way.

TONE: MANAGE YOUR WAKE

Meet Terrance

Terrance sat down with Sharon, his HR business partner, to plan for his next all-hands meeting. As the head of manufacturing for the engineering company, he had committed to holding quarterly meetings with all four hundred employees in his organization to share updates. Sharon had the results of the annual employee engagement survey. She wanted to review them with Terrance to see if they contained anything that could inform their planning for the next meeting.

While much of the survey was positive, there was a series of comments about Terrance's presence that caught his attention:

- "Terrance has not built rapport with staff beyond his direct reports. He can seem a bit aloof."

- "He needs to better communicate the vision and purpose of what we do day to day—he needs to rally the troops with more enthusiasm. Instead, he often appears like a talking head up on stage."

- "He's always extremely composed. He maintains a calm demeanor, especially under fire. This is a strength but it can also make him hard to read."

Terrance thought about previous all-hands meetings and how at ease he had felt in front of the room. Could it be that his natural comfort was conveying the wrong message? If that was the case, how could he own the room without compromising his natural style?

What Tone Do You Set and Are You Resonating with Others?

Terrance, like Patricia, wants to be at the top of his game and looks for ways to improve. The feedback from the engagement survey actually didn't surprise him. Earlier in his career, a manager had told him that his presence was hindered by his unapproachability. He had taken the feedback seriously and worked hard to improve it. What he now realized in Sharon's office was that he had focused on conveying more openness and willingness to engage with his direct reports but hadn't considered how to do the same for the people beyond that immediate circle. While he was in Signature Voice in his smaller group, his presence slid to driving voice with larger audiences. He was unable to maintain a voice for others in those larger forums. What he now pondered was how he could translate his approachability to a much larger audience. How could be sure he resonated with people several layers down in the organization in these all-hands meetings?

Once you have more clarity around your energy, your cues, and what restores you, you then need to recognize the *wake* you have within your organization. Many executives are not aware of the tremendous ripple effect their nonverbal energy and cues have throughout a company. The more senior you become, the more visible you are, and the deeper and broader the waves you send into the organization. People will read into the most subtle things about your energy—the way you position your feet when you're in front of the room at a town hall meeting or where you sit when you come into a skip-level meeting. In response, they might feel either engaged or dismayed. This can have a tremendous impact on your effectiveness as a leader and must be managed.

TONE: ACTION STEPS

There are three steps to effectively manage the tone you set. First, you must recognize that your tone affects others. Second, calibrate your energy to match the situation. Third, create physical rituals that help you maintain your composure or dial up your energy when necessary.

Recognize That Tone Is Contagious

As with all parts of Signature Voice conditioning, awareness comes first. Once you recognize that tone is contagious and reflect on how your mood may be affecting others, you will be able to calibrate and adjust it to appropriately. One of our favorite tenets on emotional resonance comes from Daniel Goleman's research and work on emotional intelligence. In *Primal Leadership*, a book he coauthored with Annie McKee and Richard Boyatzis, the authors state, "Quite simply, in any human group the leader has maximal power to sway everyone's emotions . . . How well leaders manage their moods and affect everyone else's mood, then, becomes not just a private matter, but a factor in how well a business will do."[6] What Goleman, McKee, and Boyatzis highlight is a phenomenon we see every day—that the mood of an organization starts at the top. Whether you are the CEO of a company, the head of a functional area or practice, or the senior person on a team, you set a tone that is then cascaded down through the organization.

One of our senior clients decided to leave the organization where he had worked for years. It was a place he cared deeply about and it was a tough decision. But ultimately, he was unhappy with the new CEO and the tone he set: "We all assume our roles are about the big decisions we make. But in the end, I'm leaving because of all the small things our CEO did and did not do: did he say 'Hi' or not, which meetings did he choose to attend or not, did he remember to acknowledge the team for working all weekend or not. It was all the small things he didn't do and the impact on my team that was a dealbreaker in the end." As this client's experience shows, leaders have a tremendous responsibility for managing their energy and the vibes they give off.

There's probably no better example of the importance of tone than the infamous 1960 debate between John Kennedy and Richard Nixon. In some ways, perhaps, this debate created the over-emphasis on style and spin we see today in American politics. Nonetheless, it demonstrates an important lesson in how a leader can affect followers through nonverbal cues and tone. Kayla Webley recounted the story in a *Time Magazine* article:

> *It's now common knowledge that without the nation's first tele-vised debate—fifty years ago Sunday—Kennedy would never have been president . . . What happened after the two candidates took the stage is a familiar tale. Nixon, pale and underweight from a recent hospitalization, appeared sickly and sweaty, while Kennedy appeared calm and confident. As the story goes, those who lis-tened to the debate on the radio thought Nixon had won. But those listeners were in the minority. By 1960, 88 percent of Ameri-can households had televisions—up from just 11 percent the de-cade before. The number of viewers who tuned in to the debate has been estimated as high as 74 million, by the Nielsen of the day,* Broadcast Magazine. *Those that watched the debate on TV thought Kennedy was the clear winner. Many say Kennedy won the election that night.*[7]

The tone Kennedy set that night was that of a leader. He con-vinced viewers simply through his energy that he had what it takes to be president.

Calibrate Your Energy

Terrance's natural composure was tremendously valuable in times of crisis. The team counted on his unruffled energy. They felt con-fident he would lead the way to a more stable place. But in every-day moments, this equanimity was translated as aloofness and disconnection.

Especially in larger venues, such as the all-hands meeting, the tendency toward composed energy made it difficult for an exec-utive like Terrance to connect with a larger audience. His staff ended up leaving the meeting feeling even more distant from their

FIGURE 5-1

Energy spectrum

Energy

Composed _____Expressive

(Often interpreted as aloof, distant, cold)   (Often interpreted as overemotional, too involved)

leader. Ironically, this is the exact opposite of what Terrance intended when he set up the quarterly meetings.

Think of your energy as a dimmer switch on a light. At one extreme there is darkness or composure and at the other end there is bright light, which is full expression (see figure 5-1). All people have a natural tendency toward one end or the other. The key is to be able to adjust depending on the situation, dialing the dimmer switch brighter or darker. In moments of crisis, when everyone is panicking, you want to dim your energy toward composure. In everyday business situations, when you need to rally the troops or motivate people to achieve an audacious goal, you need to turn the energy up toward expression.

As Terrance's story shows, there is a risk to both extremes. Terrance's composure was interpreted as disengaged and unapproachable. Someone like John, who naturally tends toward the expressive end, runs the risk of being interpreted as overemotional or even melodramatic. (See "How Did Terri and John Manage Their Wake?" to see how both John and Terri managed their tendency toward expressiveness.)

For the all-hands meeting, Terrance needs to move closer to expression while staying in a range of his authentic style. If not, in a larger venue like this one, his natural composure will be misunderstood and perceived as driving voice rather than Signature Voice. The question we asked Terrance to consider was: "Is your energy congruent with the conviction you have about the business or vision?" Terrance held deep conviction about the direction the group should take. By infusing more expression and energy into his delivery, he realized he was being more authentic.

HOW DID TERRI AND JOHN MANAGE THEIR WAKE?

Terri and John both realized that their tendency was toward the expressive end of the spectrum. For Terri, her natural expressiveness was in line with the passion she brought to the organization. She could see, however, that when her excitement and dedication got cranked up, she expressed anger and judgment rather than enthusiasm. What had been a core strength for her turned into a detracting disadvantage.

John saw himself as someone who was emotionally intelligent and able to read others well. However, when requests for his time became too much and he got overwhelmed, he felt further pushed toward the end of the spectrum. He became overemotional and defensive. He pushed back on the requests, flagging problems but devoting little time or energy to provide solutions.

By working on their composure, and keeping their expressiveness in check, they both made gains toward Signature Voice.

Calibrating along the continuum of composure and expression is especially important for executives who are highly visible, manage large teams of people, or are in roles where making a strong first impression counts. As Terrance's experience shows, how you manage your proximity and distance is critical. On the one hand, a leader must be connected and feel approachable; and on the other hand, the leader needs to maintain an appropriate level of objective distance.

If you orient toward a more composed presence, you must consider ways to bring more of yourself to situations so that people feel they are connecting with a human being. It's incredible how something as simple as a smile can impact how a team feels when they are in the presence of a senior executive. If you are more expressive, you need to manage how transparent you are with your emotions. Being an open book can give the impression of intimacy, something that can make others feel uncomfortable or lose confidence in you as a leader.

Create Physical Rituals

Knowing whether you tend toward expressiveness or composure, you can prepare yourself for situations where you might get pushed to one extreme or the other and make adjustments. Terrance now knows that before he presents to large audiences, he needs to put aside his "grace under fire" composure and dial up the expression. To do this, he turns to music. Terrance is a huge Broadway fan, and there is a key line in the musical *Les Misérables* that inspires him: "When the beating of your heart echoes the beating of the drums." He plays the song on his iPod right before a major presentation. Music is powerful way to change our physical state. This is why so many successful athletes include listening to music as part of their pregame ritual. Michael Phelps could be found sitting by himself with headphones on before every Olympics match.[8]

For those, like Patricia, who risk becoming too emotional, physical rituals might include breathing exercises or rituals that ground you physically, as Patricia did when she anchored her feet into the floor. This helped her to regain composure and proceed forward.

Rituals like these help to manage your nerves, something that no one is immune to. All leaders have situations or audiences that challenge their nerves and put them on edge. This is a common response to high stakes and not a weakness. Take Bill Russell, arguably one of the best players in NBA history, a five-time winner of the NBA Most Valuable Player Award, and twelve-time All Star. He is often credited for being the key reason the Celtics won a historic eleven NBA Championships. Despite his tremendous success, it was well known that Russell threw up before every game. Even at the top of his field, he felt nervous before going on the court.[9] Michael Jordan was known to calm his nerves by putting on his University of North Carolina shorts under his Bulls shorts.[10] Physical rituals matter, and top players and leaders alike need to find ways to create and institutionalize them.

VISIBILITY: THE IMPORTANCE OF BEING SEEN

Meet Doris

Doris closed the door to her office. She needed time to think. As head of corporate strategy for a technology company, she knew this was a big year for her—Marcus, the CEO, and the board were counting on her to craft their growth strategy for the next five years. This was her second year in the position, and the first had been tough as she took the helm of the function and tried to stabilize the team. Now, with a strong team in place, she knew she could afford to delegate more to her direct reports so that she could now focus on the truly big, strategic questions at hand.

One of the things on her mind was the advice she got from one of her fellow executive team members when she first moved into the role: she needed to be sure she was connected to the key players in their industry, plugged into the latest innovations, and out there in the marketplace networking with the right people. Doris knew that she should spend more time building these critical connections, but somehow this always fell to the bottom of her to-do list. Meeting annual objectives and responding to real-time requests from the executive team kept her busy enough. And it wasn't just external relationships she needed. Crafting the five-year plan meant that she needed input from key functional leaders and would need to work her internal network to do so.

Doris thought about Joanna, one of her peers and a master at strategic networking. She had always considered her a political machine, adept at knowing a lot of people and getting what she needed, but she often wondered just how sincere it all was.

Who Needs to See You?

Another key component of physical conditioning is managing your visibility. This means being intentional and thoughtful about who you need to be in the physical presence of. For some leaders, this means walking the halls where their teams sit or making use of videoconferencing, especially when teams are co-located across building, states, or even countries. For others, like Doris, the strategic nature of her role meant that she had to be at the forefront of the latest thinking and trends in her industry as well as connecting with internal stakeholders.

Doris got the promotion in large part because she had worked hard on herself as a leader. She had a Signature Voice and understood the positive ripple effect she had on others. In this new role, however, she was running the risk of making a big mistake: staying too locked into the day-to-day deliverables and requests when she needed to be seen by and in contact with others. Her presence had slid to supportive voice: she was meeting the daily needs of others but not truly fulfilling the ultimate vision for her role—that she define the next frontier for the organization. It was time for Doris to be in regular contact with other people inside and outside of his organization.

Doris needs to take an important step, one that she recognizes is important but has not yet set out to do: broaden the group of people she is in the physical presence of and increase her visibility. This will allow her to gain greater support for her ideas and elicit critical input from others that will shape the future of her company.

Those that slide to driving voice aren't immune to problems in this area either. They tend to focus only on the senior-level relationships and fail to make themselves visible to the rest of the organization.

BEING VISIBLE: ACTION STEPS

Because time is always of essence, the first step to increasing your visibility and physical presence is to get clear on who you need to be in the presence of. Once you are clear on this, then you can think about how to garner those relationships in a reciprocal and authentic way.

Map Out Key Influencers

To manage your visibility you need to understand who the key influencers are. Doris needed to ask herself who could support, add to, influence, or help shape the five-year growth strategy. This required brainstorming beyond the usual suspects she felt most comfortable speaking to and thinking more broadly across the enterprise and beyond it. Once she had a list of people with whom she needed to touch base, she had to consider the best ways to make contact with them and through what mechanism. For the key influencers—those who could make or break the plan—it made sense to meet with them one on one. For those whose support would be helpful but not necessary, she could attend func-

---

HOW DID JOHN INCREASE HIS VISIBILITY?

Learning how to increase his visibility was a big opportunity for John, given that he had received feedback that the partners outside of the Chicago office knew who he was but did not really know what he stood for. How could he share with others who he was as a leader of the firm, not just as someone heading one office? What opportunities could he seize to get in front of partners who didn't know him as well? How could he demonstrate his areas of expertise so that others would know when to reach out for his counsel? John realized that increasing his visibility wasn't about bragging, it was about providing his perspective on key issues to others in the firm. By increasing his voice for self and putting himself out there more, he wasn't being a show-off—he was connecting with others.

---

tional staff meetings, presenting her ideas and getting input from a larger group at one time. (To see how John handled this issue, see "How Did John Increase His Visibility?")

In their *Harvard Business Review* article, "How Leaders Create and Use Networks," Herminia Ibarra and Mark Hunter identify three types of networks:

- *Operational:* People, usually those in your immediate function, you need to accomplish your assigned, routine tasks.

- *Personal:* Relationships with people outside your organization who can help you with personal advancement.

- *Strategic:* People outside your control who will enable you to reach key organizational objectives.

Ibarra and Hunter observe, "When aspiring leaders do not believe that networking is one of the most important requirements of their new jobs, they will not allocate enough time and effort to see it pay off."[11] Most people are smart about building the first two networks. However, having a Signature Voice requires that you cultivate the third as well. Reaching beyond your usual realm builds your physical presence and visibility as a leader. As Ibarra and Hunter say, "When managers begin the delicate transition from functional manager to business leader, they must start to concern themselves with broad strategic issues . . . Strategic networking plugs the aspiring leader into a set of relationships and information sources that collectively embody the power to achieve personal and organizational goals."[12] For those whose presence slides to supportive voice this means getting out of your shell and reaching out to people at the top of the organization and outside of it. For those who tend toward driving voice, you must recognize that being seen by just the most senior levels of the organization is not enough. You need to increase your visibility with all groups, especially influential peers.

FIGURE 5-2

Define your network

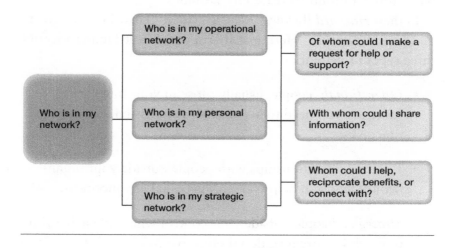

DRILL

Identify Key Influencers

Many of our clients have found Ibarra and Hunter's three-network framework useful and asked us to help them make it actionable. In figure 5-2, you'll see how we've taken the framework and created a drill to help individuals more clearly define their networks and create a plan to build them.

Go through each question and make a note of who is in each of your networks and how you can enhance the relationship. By the end of the exercise, you should have three to five people in each bucket as part of your existing network. Then think of at least two new people to add to each network. To establish a connection with these people, make use of both your voice for self and your voice for others:

- **Make requests (voice for self):** To build your network you need to ask for things. Effectively and confidently ask for referrals or information. Do this in a way that feels authentic and positive.

- **Share information (voice for others):** Pay attention to what other people need and share information that will help them meet their goals.

- **Make it mutually beneficial (both voice for others and for self):** Approach networking in an authentic, values-driven way. Reciprocate any favors you receive by sharing information, making introductions, or acting as a referral.

Keep It Real

Building your network or increasing your visibility can be especially tough for people who fear that they will appear mercenary or ingratiating. Certainly, there is a risk of overdoing it. Most people can sense when you are reaching out to them solely for your own motives or advancement. This behavior can work against your presence, rather than for it. Instead, you need to seek out a dialogue or an exchange in which the relationship becomes a two-way street, not just you looking out for yourself. Doris felt true conviction about the direction the company was heading in. When she reached out to counterparts in other functional areas, she had thought through what each stakeholder stood to gain from this vision and conveyed that in an authentic way. Rather than irking these key influencers, she engaged them.

Executives like Doris who resist "politics" or don't prioritize being visible risk becoming invisible to the rest of the organization. Watch out for the two ends of the continuum. On one end, a very savvy communicator and political navigator in an organization can project too much polish if he lacks authenticity and relies too heavily on his charm to influence people. He may give a chameleon-like impression, that he'll say whatever is necessary to get the job done. On the other end of the spectrum is the good "soldier" who is naturally supportive of others but is only visible in a reactive way, when he absolutely needs to be. In the middle of this continuum is the sweet spot where you make yourself physically present in an authentic way—not because you

FIGURE 5-3

Visibility in the four quadrants

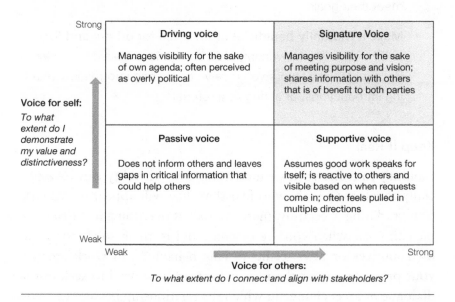

Strong

Driving voice

Manages visibility for the sake of own agenda; often perceived as overly political

Signature Voice

Manages visibility for the sake of meeting purpose and vision; shares information with others that is of benefit to both parties

Voice for self:
To what extent do I demonstrate my value and distinctiveness?

Passive voice

Does not inform others and leaves gaps in critical information that could help others

Supportive voice

Assumes good work speaks for itself; is reactive to others and visible based on when requests come in; often feels pulled in multiple directions

Weak

Weak   Strong

Voice for others:
To what extent do I connect and align with stakeholders?

have to, but because you want to. Share information and offer help in a mutually beneficial way. That is Signature Voice (see figure 5-3).

WHAT TO REMEMBER

- Energy is what people see when they look at you. It is more than just your "book cover" or how you dress; it also includes your nonverbal cues and the vibes you give off. As with all the components of ACE, it is part of an integrated system. The energy you convey impacts your mind and your communications.

- To physically condition for Signature Voice, you must identify and learn your physical cues—when you are in top shape and when your presence starts sliding. Physical cues are great indicators of your presence.

- All leaders, especially more senior ones, have a ripple effect on the organization. Your energy sets the tone for your unit, department, or function.

- To resonate with others, you need to manage how composed and expressive you are. Some situations require you lean toward one end of the spectrum or the other.

- To manage your visibility, you need to identify a strategic network of people you should be in the physical presence of in an authentic, reciprocal way.

CHAPTER SIX

WHAT'S NEXT?

Eighteen months after we stopped working with John, he celebrated his promotion to managing partner for North America. He had been at the firm for over eight years, and it was a momentous occasion. It seemed like only yesterday that Roger had shared the news with him over coffee that it was far from a slam dunk that he would get the promotion. In the e-mail announcing his promotion, Roger and the other managing partners were generous with praise: "John has a unique combination of skills. He brings a relationship focus to an uncompromising pursuit of results on behalf of our people and our clients. He is an invaluable asset to our firm." John's innate abilities—empathy and thoughtfulness—are fundamental to his success with colleagues and clients. He is known, both inside the firm and to clients, as a trusted adviser.

True to form, John is motivated by his strong relationships with clients, team members, and his fellow partners. As a result, he has been able to lead the North America practice through unprecedented change, which in turn has resulted in top-line results that have exceed original goals. The most senior firm leaders are closely watching the North America practice to see what can be learned and replicated in the other regions. There is even early talk of John taking on a global leadership role down the line. John is frank about his continued struggles to balance the competing demands of life at the firm, but he has clearly made great strides in establishing clear priorities and boundaries. While thoughtful and collaborative at the core, he has learned to adapt when the situation demands it and be decisive about firm issues, taking a stand and proactively setting direction. Even at his most assertive, however, his empathetic style prevails so that he never loses his authenticity.

Terri recently completed her tenure as leader of the enterprise-wide initiative at the bank where she works. The project required intense cooperation and collaboration with IT, sales, and finance. It was an enormous success, due in large part to Terri's leadership. Terri's relentless drive to push the project forward was undoubt-edly a critical component. So, too, was her facility with recogniz-ing the moments when others should lead and moving aside to encourage that. Her boss, Sean, was sincerely pleased when he heard Terri's peers demonstrate appreciation for how she increas-ingly sought their input over the course of the project. While Sean had tapped Terri for this role because of her ability to be decisive, confident, and results oriented, he had also worried about some of Terri's sharper edges and her ability to "play nice in the sandbox" with others. At presentations to the C-suite, the CEO commented that she was pleased to see Terri spend more time listening and exploring options in a more consultative manner. Even the fact that she let others on the team do most of the presenting after she kicked it off was a testament to how far she had come and matured into a more executive presence. While she is still a take-charge type of individual, her ability to do so in a more inclusive way increased her equity with the C-Suite and her peers both in-side and outside of the sales function. The word around the com-pany is that she's next in line for the SVP of Marketing role.

Both Terri and John found their Signature Voice in their new roles. John's signature is to be an empathetic collaborative leader who can drive results for himself, his clients, and his firm. Terri's signature is to be a results-oriented leader who can motivate and inspire others to the end zone. While both made great strides with their leadership presence, notice how different their presence is. One of the hallmarks of Signature Voice is authenticity. By conditioning from the inside out, Terri and John each found a voice that was effective and truly their own.

One of the best parts of coaching and teaching Signature Voice through the years has been the updates, calls, and e-mails we've received from clients years later. Being part of the celebration when a leaders gets a major promotion or completes a critical organizational initiative has been one of the most rewarding parts of our work.

SIGNATURE VOICE IS A JOURNEY

Think of any star athlete—Michael Jordan in basketball, Chris Evert in tennis, Tiger Woods in golf—these are athletes who have been at the top of their game. Once they reach the pinnacle of their sport, they don't sit back. They have a conditioning regimen: every day they practice, they prepare themselves, they get better. Even with skills that inspire awe in others, they are conscious and intentional about their sport, not asleep and on autopilot. They are always looking for that extra edge. Great leaders are similarly intentional about building their presence.

As you've learned throughout this book, the behaviors that comprise a Signature Voice are individual to every person and are acquired with intentional practice. No one is born with them. They are not handed out as you make the transition into firm leader or SVP. Anyone, at any level, can have them. But developing a Signature Voice is a lifelong commitment. You aren't going to find after reading this book that your voice is permanently changed. In fact, even when you build a Signature Voice, you have to continue to work at maintaining it. Forever.

While this can sound daunting, the conditioning for Signature Voice can be fun, invigorating, and fulfilling. It reminds us to be aware and present to ourselves and others. It allows us to turn off autopilot and think more deeply about the choice we have. But it's important to recognize that rather than being an end goal, Signature Voice is an evolution.

In their book *Leadership Agility*, Bill Joiner and Stephen Josephs divide the leadership population into five levels, from Expert to Synergist. *Synergists*, the highest level, are those who think about the organization holistically, wear a strategic hat, and have aligned to their life purpose. Their leadership presence is one that has moved well beyond being assertive and driving or accommodating and supportive. In fact, they've achieved the Signature Voice that integrates their assertive and accommodating sides and are agile in using both styles. They are able to be appropriate to the situation at hand. Joiner and Josephs' research shows that only 1 percent of leaders have reached that level.[1] That is a small fraction of the leadership population. For the remaining 99 percent, this is an ongoing process, and we encourage you to enjoy the ride.

After you use ACE to enhance your Signature Voice, there are three ways you can continue to enhance and condition your voice:

- Return to ACE when new situations cause your presence to slide.

- Align, motivate, and inspire your organization.

- Lead with purpose.

ADDRESS BACKSLIDES

Terri and John went on to celebrate many more gains in their presence—to own larger rooms. Along the way, they embraced the journey and accepted that it wasn't always a linear path. In fact, Terri and John recognized that they were not immune to backsliding.

A year after his promotion, John called us. He was feeling himself backslide to old behaviors—not voicing his opinion, taking on the brunt of the work instead of setting priorities, letting some of the partners' issues take precedent over moving forward with the plan he had laid out. There was talk that his firm might be acquired by a larger consulting organization, and John feared that he wasn't going to be able to integrate into that behemoth of an organization, which had a drastically different culture and market approach. John had been assured that his position was secure and in fact had been given a greater scope of responsibility. The acquiring firm was based in Europe, and its leadership saw John's group as a strong beachhead into the North America geography. But with an increasingly complex set of internal and external stakeholders, declining morale on his team, and lack of clarity about the future, John could feel old vulnerabilities emerge in his now larger role.

As for Terri, within six months of the success of the enterprisewide initiative, she got the promotion she wanted. She was now the SVP of Marketing. Soon after the rounds of congratulations and the move to her new corner office, she realized she'd inherited a mess. Communication between sales and marketing was severely strained. Sales reps didn't buy into the marketing plans and struggled to interpret the brand messages for the financial products. Finance had whittled away at marketing's resources in an effort to cut costs, leaving the brand teams strapped and unable to do their jobs. Terri's first inclination was to get on the phone with all the brand managers and threaten them to shape up or ship out. She knew if she pushed hard enough, she could convince the CEO and COO to just let her wipe the slate clean and start over with a new team she could call her own. As she pored over the data and heard more from her direct reports, she felt herself precipitously sliding to driving voice, losing sight of her voice for others.

The key to effective leadership presence is not only the ability to attain it but to increase your awareness to know when your presence is starting to slide. Circumstances change—new business requirements, new roles, new direct reports—and your presence must be flexible enough to change with them. When you notice, as John and Terri did, that you are starting to slide, you need to recognize the triggers—the specific events, people, or circumstances that are causing you to backslide, and then correct your course. Those who slide to supportive voice have a set of common triggers. For John, it was the increasing demands, ambiguity of his role, and the decreasing morale on his team. For someone who slides to driving voice, the triggers are likely to be different. In Terri's case, she was activated by the fear that results were waning.

Start by being aware of the life events that can cause you to lose focus on either voice for self or voice for others. If you catch the signs early enough you can then correct your course. Table 6-1 shows some common trigger events and signs.

When you recognize one of these signs, it's important to catch yourself before you slide further. For those who slide to driving voice, it means bringing some additional focus back to voice for others while maintaining your strong voice for self. For those who slide to supportive voice, it means bringing some consciousness to your voice for self while staying attuned to others. Like a seasoned golfer who intuitively understands that his swing is off before he completes it and takes a step back to correct it, you need to return to the basics and take the time to be sure you are on the right track.

Those who have ever picked up a sport or musical instrument know that when they get rusty or hit a wall, they need to go back to the basic drills. A piano player will go back to practicing scales. A basketball player will return to taking shots from different court positions. A golfer will go back to practicing swings without actually hitting the ball. They do these things for two reasons. First, returning to the basics helps to simplify the situation you're facing. Second, these drills tap into the muscle memory you have developed. When you've practiced something enough, you can

TABLE 6-1

Trigger events and signs of backsliding

Trigger event	Signs of slide to supportive voice	Signs of slide to driving voice
Promotion	• You spend an inordinate amount of time listening to stakeholders or direct reports without articulating your own vision. • You feel the need to get into the details of the work in order to prove competence in your role.	• You act rashly, feeling an urgency to make changes or start from scratch. • You consider only the data and consult with a select few rather than reaching out to a broader audience. • You straddle the responsibilities of your new role without letting go of your old ones.
Reorganization	• You hem and haw about articulating a direction for your team or organization, afraid to put a stake in the ground. • You get sucked into the emotional turmoil of staff dealing with changes.	• You set a unilateral vision and direction without gathering input from others. • You feel a need to make changes fast.
New boss	• You are overly responsive to requests and demands. • You feel you must show deference.	• You feel a need to get ample face time.
Lagging performance	• You emphasize the effort over the results.	• You emphasize results at all cost.

remember how to do it with some simple reminders. Likewise, ACE is the drill that you go back to when you need to adjust your presence.

John's main trigger was the increasing workload and complexity presented by the potential acquisition. Table 6-2 shows how he corrected his slide.

For Terri, when she became SVP of Marketing, her slide was triggered by the lagging results she was seeing in the organization. This went against the grain of one of her fundamental values—achievement and success. When Terri felt herself sliding to driving voice, she used the tactics laid out in table 6-3 to get back on track.

TABLE 6-2

John's tactics for achieving Signature Voice

Assumptions	• Gained clarity on the opportunities for him, his team, and the firm coming out of the potential acquisition. • Checked his assumptions with other senior leaders and got involved in the acquisition discussions.
Communication strategies	• Communicated consistently and as openly as possible with partners and staff. • Framed the potential organizational changes for his team in a way that helped them see the opportunities and priorities, not just the downsides and uncertainty. • Proactively shaped priorities and responded to requests accordingly.
Energy	• Took care of himself physically by practicing meditation and doing yoga to reduce his anxiety. • Made himself visible to those involved in the acquisition discussions.

TABLE 6-3

Terri's tactics for achieving Signature Voice

Assumptions	• Told herself: Results are important, but I won't see them overnight. It's taken some time to get into this mess, and I don't need to turn it around overnight. • Recognized that her highest value—achievement—was not equally held by everyone else in the organization. She needed to drive results without demoralizing the team.
Communication strategies	• Listened, listened, and listened some more to key stake-holders, including those in the field. • Didn't focus solely on what needed to be done but balanced that with the acknowledgment of what had been accomplished to date. • Framed the challenge to get to better results through a team effort, not just through her own sheer will.
Energy	• Set a tone of realistic optimism to keep the team moving forward while managing her disappointment with the present.

At the end of working with coaching clients, we ask them to create a one-page table they can look at every day to remind them what assumptions, communication strategies, and energy drives their personal best. One of our clients told us that even now, many years after coaching, he still pulls up that page when he finds himself in a challenging situation.

ALIGN, MOTIVATE, AND INSPIRE

Leaders who have found their Signature Voice have a greater ability to align, motivate, and inspire others, especially during times of organizational change and uncertainty. The more senior you become, the more often your role requires that you deliver organizational news, decisions, or policies that impact a significant number of people. These moments present the greatest challenge and the greatest opportunity for your leadership presence and your ability to be authentic and connect with others. In these situations, your voice is the voice of the organization, and what you believe, what you say, and how you show up physically have a tremendous impact on others.

One of our clients, Sally, had been a rising star in her Wall Street firm since the day she arrived. She was now an executive and known for her ability to make tough decisions and motivate others to follow through. Those who worked with her—superiors, direct reports, and peers alike—appreciated her approachability and her ability to build rapport with others. Her role required that she often interface with other divisions, which she did with aplomb. The senior leaders relied on her as a strong representative of the organization to external stakeholders as well.

Sally reached out for coaching when the firm went through a major reorganization that disproportionately affected her unit. Her employees were frustrated and concerned about the future. While the changes were unpleasant, she believed in the business reasons for them and even helped to shape the restructuring. Her boss had asked her to lead the group through this transition, handling the internal issues as well as external communications with key constituents. She accepted the charge but reached out for coaching to help her figure out how to best approach the role.

Sally was already capable in her Signature Voice. She had both a strong voice for self and voice for others and knew how to use them. However, she was starting to sense a slide to supportive voice. Others around her may not have noticed anything—she was seasoned enough to be able to manage her physical presence and exude composure. But internally, Sally felt uneasy. She found that her sympathy for the employees' sentiments about the reorganization was affecting her view on what she needed to do. Using the ACE model, we worked with Sally to set assumptions that served her during this time of change, hone her messaging, and condition her energy. Table 6-4 shows how Sally proactively used

TABLE 6-4

How Sally aligned, motivated, and inspired

Assumptions	• Gained clarity on her own viewpoint on the change so that she could speak authentically to the rest of the organization • Articulated a vision for what the change would accomplish and what the future state would look like

Communication strategies	• Crafted a communication plan that incorporated voice for self and voice for others:
	  — Acknowledged the impact of the change and the challenges it presented (voice for others)
	  — Shared her commitment to the change and painted a vision and way forward (voice for self)
	• Offered to talk with anyone throughout the change
	• Determined which forums were most appropriate to communicate her message

Energy	• Increased her visibility across the organization • Set an appropriate tone and attitude toward the change; used a more serious tone when acknowledging the impact the change would have but also ended with an optimistic tone when she shared her conviction and vision • Ensured she was accessible to peers and staff so they felt heard and included in the process

the ACE model to motivate and inspire others and ultimately lead a successful change initiative.

Warren Buffett once said, "Success is really doing what you love and doing it well. It's as simple as that. Really getting to do what you love to do everyday—that's really the ultimate luxury."[2] When you are able to find alignment between what you love to do and what your organization does, you are more fully able to use your Signature Voice. In a similar vein, Rhonda Mims, the president of the ING Foundation and senior vice president at ING Americas said, "Pick a place where you can take your whole self to work."[3] (But sometimes finding that sweet spot won't be possible; see "Knowing When It's Time to Leave.")

KNOWING WHEN IT'S TIME TO LEAVE

The reality is that sometimes identifying Signature Voice and the new capacity and clarity it brings can also surface tough choices for leaders. Some individuals find that the Signature Voice they've worked so hard to identify is at odds with their organization. We've seen clients who have done lots of twisting and turning to try to get their values to fit with that of their organization. This is likely to cause you discomfort in the long run when the seams start to come undone. Be honest with yourself if there is a mismatch.

A client of ours, Mary, had been a stand-out senior analyst when she left her firm a few years back. Her life partner had gotten a job in another city, so Mary took some time off. Now, they had decided to move back to the east coast, and she was offered a position back at her firm. Mary was excited about coming back. It was a place where she had learned and grown a lot. She thought of it as a place that respected people's contributions and promoted work-life balance. In her first year back, Mary thrived. She managed a service team and was once again at the top of her game in terms of developing her team and meeting goals. At the same time, she had access to senior management to help shape the direction of the delivery center for the firm.

A year into her second tenure, the firm shifted its strategy to heavily focus on what could be delivered through the service centers. Mary found herself in the new "hot" area of the firm and, while exciting, the change was hard. She worked more hours. She had less access to senior people. Her team's morale was fading. And as a result, she became increasingly frustrated. Mary decided to talk directly with senior leaders about whether the increased stress level was a short-term situation. In these conversations, she came to realize that the firm's culture and way of operating was fundamentally changing. The senior leadership team, spurred by an aggressive board of directors, expected a faster pace and greater commitment from everyone. Mary wondered whether she could get comfortable with this new firm, whether she could let go of the firm that she had once been so fond of. She was at a crossroads.

Mary's situation highlights the same challenge Sally experienced around leadership presence. How do you communicate, not to mention even align and rally others, when you yourself have not yet bought in or when the decision feels like it flies in the face of your values?

Unfortunately, Mary wasn't able to achieve the alignment she needed to motivate others. She had reached a point where the organization's culture was at odds with her presence. Over short periods of time, a leader can live with such a discrepancy or find enough intersection points to handle interim decisions that she may not agree with. But we've found if the misalignment occurs over long durations and with high frequency, it becomes unsustainable—either the individual suffers because she can't be authentic or the organization pays the price because the leader is not living up to her potential. When you're caught in a misalignment, it's difficult to be a source of motivation for others. In Mary's case, her own performance, which had never been in question, started sliding, and the level of stress she was experiencing was magnified. Because the potential for misalignment with the organization increases the more senior you become and the more often you're asked to be the voice for the organization, it's important for leaders to continually assess the intersection between self and organization. In the end, the right thing for Mary was to leave her firm and find a new opportunity elsewhere.

DRILL

Find Intersection Points Between You and Your Organization

As Sally's experience shows, one of the greatest challenges of presence at the most senior levels is feeling that you can get up in front of the organization and speak with authenticity. Many leaders struggle to stay on corporate message while delivering a message to their teams, divisions, or even the media that feels like their own.

When your voice for self is the voice of the organization, it is critical that you find alignment between you and the organization before you can go out and motivate others. Figure 6-1 is an exercise designed to help you better understand yourself and the organization in order to find the intersection points. Answer the questions on either side of the chart and then note where there is overlap. These are the points on which you should focus. They will give you the strength you need to lead others through tough times.

LEAD WITH PURPOSE

Finding your Signature Voice is an incredibly rewarding experience. When you become more competent in both your voice for self and voice for others, you expand the possibilities of what you

FIGURE 6-1

Find the intersection points between you and your organization

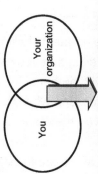

You	Points of intersection	Your organization
What experiences to date have made you successful? What are you most passionate about or proud of?		What experiences to date have made your organization successful? What is the organization passionate about or proud of?
What future opportunities most excite you within your functional area, your organization, and in the marketplace?		What future opportunities must your organization capture for its long-term sustainability and growth?
What are you/would you like to be recognized for within your organization or in the marketplace?		What is your organization recognized for externally in the marketplace? What about in your functional area?
What contribution or impact would you like to make for your organization?		What contribution or impact does your organization make in the industry or world at large?
What values do you hold most near and dear?		What organizational values do you most want to exemplify and uphold?

can achieve. We've seen clients, with their increased capability to influence and navigate bigger platforms and a variety of situations and audiences, find the room to ask the bigger questions about purpose, vision, and living an authentic life.

We worked with a client, Carmen, who was a director at an investment bank. When we first met her, she had already achieved great success because of her technical expertise in business deals, but she was hitting a ceiling, in large part because of her tendency to slide to driving voice. She understood financial instruments better than anyone at the firm, and people regularly turned to her for advice. While she had command of her area of expertise, she had the tendency to approach interactions in a transactional manner. She always wanted to be "the expert" and found it difficult to step out of that role. Many of her colleagues described their dealings with her as awkward. They felt they couldn't ever really get to know who she was as a person when she wasn't acting the expert. We worked with Carmen to uncover what was happening for her. It turned out that her slide was the result of a faulty assumption. She believed that she would be most valuable to the firm by focusing on the technical details and that she needed to continually prove her deep knowledge. What she failed to realize was that her expertise was already highly valued, and her insistence on repeatedly demonstrating it was hindering her. Over the course of six months, Carmen worked tirelessly to reset her assumptions, hone her communication skills, and manage her energy. Most importantly, she put down her "technical mask" and started showing more of herself. She began to relax when she accepted that she didn't need to be the know-it-all in order to win her colleague's trust. She was relieved to learn she had earned her right to be at the table long ago. Now her colleagues wanted to forge a stronger relationship with her. Carmen felt greater self-confidence and began revealing more of her true self. Her colleagues were surprised to find that behind all that technical brilliance was also a sharp-witted, funny, and caring person.

In our last coaching session with Carmen, we were reflecting on the incredible progress she made. She asked us, "What do I do now?" Confused by the question, we looked at her silently. She explained, "I feel like I have so much more capacity now. I feel like I want to really make a difference, leave a mark on others." Carmen told us that she wanted to help other women executives like herself in the organization. We encouraged her to use her newfound influence to make that happen. A year later, Carmen had put this vision into action; she had designed and implemented a new sponsorship program for rising female leaders in her firm. She tells us that she uses the Signature Voice concepts and ACE with all of them.

When you are able to have a voice and connect with others—when you find your Signature Voice—you actually become more yourself. Consider Al Gore. The question of whether or not he should have assumed the office of US president after the 2000 elections will, no doubt, be hotly contested for generations. Why did he lose? Was the process constitutional? Should Gore have stuck to his guns and seen the court battle through?

Whatever the conclusion to these questions, there's one point on which pundits agreed: Al Gore, the vice president and presidential candidate, was no beacon of leadership presence. His detractors called him robotic, unfeeling, and disconnected. Even stalwart fans admitted he was a little "reserved." His Democratic predecessor, Bill Clinton, was famous for his charisma—his ability to fill a room, his genius for making individuals he spoke with feel like they were the only people in the world who mattered—and poor Gore paled in comparison.

But fewer than five years later, a new Gore emerged. Standing before that dullest of mediums—a PowerPoint presentation—he exuded far more warmth and certainly more enthusiasm. The persona that was reintroduced through the film *An Inconvenient Truth* was a new Al Gore: an energetic, more connected leader. Attuned to his audience, he projected genuine passion for his cause. He even won the Nobel Peace Prize in 2007. This "new and improved" Al Gore showed fewer traces of the robotic behavior he was known for as VP and would-be-president.

By letting what he cared most about be the center of his work, he was able to be less mechanical and show a presence that was consistent, connected and authentic. Gore's is a transformational story, one that shows how leadership presence emerges when you speak from a place of your most heartfelt beliefs, and how someone who has earned the seemingly permanent and career-killing label "robotic" can find within a voice that feels authentic and connected.

Gore didn't try to emulate Clinton. He didn't go jogging through neighborhoods and chat up people on the street. He did what was truly unique to him: he found a voice all his own. It was a purpose that has driven him to new heights of achievement.

Once you've found your Signature Voice, you can use that platform to have an even bigger impact than before. Not only can you be better at your current role but you influence a broader sphere and infuse your work with purpose and mission.

PASSING THE BATON

Like Carmen, you may be inspired to help others find their own Signature Voice. In her vision to help other women executives, she used the Signature Voice concepts to coach others around presence. She felt energized by being part of that development and drew from it to continue to engage with her work. She told us that of all her accomplishments, she felt most rewarded and fulfilled when others told her that she had made a difference in their careers and lives. Like Carmen, if you manage others, you have the opportunity to use these frameworks to help others grow and develop as well. In the next chapter, we explain how you can support others in their Signature Voice journey.

WHAT TO REMEMBER

- One of the hallmarks of Signature Voice is authenticity. By conditioning from the inside out, you can establish a voice that is effective and truly your own. When you become more competent in your voice for self and voice for others, you expand the possibilities of what you can achieve.

- The key to effective leadership presence is not only the ability to attain it but to be aware enough to know when your presence is starting to slide. Circumstances change—new business requirements, new roles, new direct reports—and your presence must be flexible enough to change with them.

- The more senior you become, the more often your role requires that you deliver organizational news, decisions, or policies that impact a significant magnitude of people. These moments present the greatest challenge and the greatest opportunity for your leadership presence and your ability to be authentic and connect with others. Finding the alignment between yourself and the organization is a critical first step before you can motivate and inspire others.

- With increased capability to influence and navigate a variety of situations and audiences, there is more room to ask bigger questions about purpose and vision. Authentic leadership presence emerges when you speak from a place of your most heartfelt beliefs and let purpose drive your achievements.

CHAPTER SEVEN

HELPING OTHERS FIND THEIR SIGNATURE VOICE

S o far, this book has focused on how an individual leader can build a more authentic, confident, and connected leadership presence. Many of our clients, upon finding their Signature Voice, are inspired to help their direct reports and others in their organization do the same. As a manager, you can support others on their own journey toward Signature Voice. As someone's manager, mentor, or peer, you can play a critical role in supporting and accelerating the individual's growth in presence. (Also see "How Can You Shape the Organizational Conversation About Presence?")

HOW CAN YOU SHAPE THE ORGANIZATIONAL CONVERSATION ABOUT PRESENCE?

N ow that you are more aware of the true drivers of presence, you may notice that the way key people in your organization talk about presence is counterproductive or even damaging. As an individual, you may not have the power to challenge your company's culture, especially one that is particularly entrenched. But you can set an example for others and use appropriate platforms—talent reviews, career development councils, or partner election discussions—to convey the importance of leadership presence and alter the discussion. In the introduction, we talked about the most common myths that organizations perpetuate around leadership presence. Here's how you can challenge them and proactively influence your organization's culture:

Emphasize that presence is something anyone can build: In talent review discussions, it's not uncommon for someone to say, "I just don't think he has the gravitas required for the role." When this sort of comment comes up, don't let it slide. By now, you know that presence isn't something that's only available to a select few. Building bench strength begins with an open mind about what's possible for the individuals in the organization. Don't assume—or let others presume—that because someone doesn't have presence now, she can't build it.

Don't let others pigeonhole presence as an issue of appearance or communication style: When you are part of conversations about someone's presence, don't allow people to talk about the issue as if it's one-dimensional. Leadership presence is a function of three things: mind, skill, and body. Most programs emphasize the physical elements, such as how to manage your energy or use dramatic techniques. Participants are often disappointed when the changes they make don't move the needle on their presence. If your organization is offering training around presence, ask whether it will address all aspects or just one.

Create a common language: We are continually surprised—and dismayed—by how organizations address the challenge of leadership presence. Managers and HR representatives, with the best of intentions, fail to articulate what they need or expect from rising leaders and provide only vague feedback. This is a disservice to the individual and to the organization. Organizations need a common language for discussing presence. Refuse to perpetuate the common myths that presence is about how polished you are, what suit you wear, how much you resemble those in the C-suite. Instead, insist on the balance that we know and observe: people don't buy spin; they follow and respect those who bring together style and substance. Be clear, in your discussions, about what presence is. Encourage others to agree on an explicit definition. By using a shared language and framework to discuss presence, you have a far better shot at helping individual build this critical capability and create a culture in which authenticity and adaptability are both respected and cultivated.

Roger was instrumental in John's search for his Signature Voice. John was initially confused about the feedback Roger gave him. He felt that the partners were sending him a message that while he was confident and savvy enough to be an office partner, he was not confident and savvy enough to be the managing partner for North America. Roger helped John to understand, process, and interpret that feedback so it made sense. Sean was also a vital help to Terri. She heard his feedback loud and clear but she wasn't sure she agreed with it or could do anything about it. Even in her most open moments, when she was ready to address the concerns people had raised about her, she was not sure if she was going about it in the right way.

While both Terri and John could have tried to build their presence alone and would have probably made significant strides, having managers who were comfortable coaching them made their efforts much more effective. This chapter provides specific advice on how to coach and mentor people for whom presence is an issue.

THE ROLE YOU PLAY: MANAGER AS COACH

In our own work as coaches, we have seen the Signature Voice framework function not just as catalyst for greater understanding of presence and what it requires, but also as a way to help leaders get through initial inertia to action. We've had several clients tell us that after being coached with the framework, they turn around and use it in their work with their direct reports. Here's how Signature Voice can help you fulfill your role as a coach to others.

When someone is working to enhance their presence, they often grapple with the fundamental questions about how to get there:

- What message am I sending with my current presence?

- How can I improve my leadership presence in an authentic way? What should I do first?

- How do I deal with specific situations where my presence is being challenged?

- How do I know if I'm making any progress?

When you act as a manager as coach, the Signature Voice framework enables you to address each of these questions head-on in a practical and actionable way. Using it, you can:

- *Offer a clear assessment of presence:* Help your direct reports understand how their presence is currently perceived and the impact it's having.

- *Create an integrated action plan:* Help them articulate a plan to develop their presence using the ACE model.

- *Offer coaching in real time:* Help them work through specific issues and challenges along the way.

- *Celebrate growth and help overcome obstacles:* Help them recognize the successes and obstacles that are part of the process.

Offer a Clear Assessment

Receiving untarnished, candid feedback about how one is perceived can be an eye-opening experience, but it can also be intensely confusing. As a manager, you can help to clarify what the feedback means, guiding your direct report to interpret and unpack his presence and how it impacts others. By tying the feedback to the Signature Voice quadrants, you can help the leader make sense of what may feel like disjointed criticism. Feedback often comes from multiple sources and is disorganized. Trying to pull out themes can be tough for an individual who is feeling sensitive or offended about what he's hearing.

Write down the main points and map them to the four quadrants. This requires a two-step process:

1. First, make note of the positive feedback that a direct report's colleagues shared about her presence. All people have moments of Signature Voice, when they demonstrate their value and distinction while staying connected and aware of their audience. Explain to your direct report that these are the moments when she is in the zone. If colleagues haven't offered examples of these times, consider asking for them. This is extremely important, as it will help your direct report understand when her presence is working.

2. Then, look at the constructive feedback and map the rest of the points to the other presence quadrants to explain how the feedback shows where the individual slides to. Remember that some leaders may go to different quadrants, depending on the situation or with whom they are interacting, but most people have one default quadrant. Call that out.

This process of tying the feedback to the quadrants doesn't need to be complex. Simply drawing the quadrants on a sheet of paper and making the connections verbally is often enough to frame the feedback so it makes sense to the leader. It gives them a foundation and the encouragement to do something about it.

FIGURE 7-1

Feedback mapped to the presence quadrants

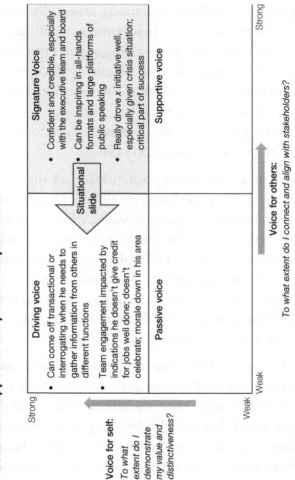

Voice for self:
To what extent do I demonstrate my value and distinctiveness?

Voice for others:
To what extent do I connect and align with stakeholders?

Driving voice

- Can come off transactional or interrogating when he needs to gather information from others in different functions
- Team engagement impacted by indications he doesn't give credit for jobs well done; doesn't celebrate; morale down in his area

Signature Voice

- Confident and credible, especially with the executive team and board
- Can be inspiring in all-hands formats and large platforms of public speaking
- Really drove x initiative well, especially given crisis situation; critical part of success

Passive voice

Supportive voice

Situational slide

Strong

Weak

Weak

Strong

Figure 7-1 presents a sample of one manager's drawing of his direct report's feedback.

In addition to clarifying the feedback, encourage the individual to continue to proactively seek additional input. Help her identify the critical stakeholders on her team or elsewhere in the organization who can give her periodic insights into her presence. This will help embolden the leader to engage others in helping her be successful rather than approach her development in isolation.

Create an Integrated Action Plan

As a manager, you can help others get started by laying out a specific action plan. This serves as a roadmap to building their presence.

Using the ACE model to create the plan provides focus and ensures that the individual is approaching presence—building voice for self and voice for others—in an integrated way rather than working on one piece at a time. Here are the steps to help develop an action plan:

1. Walk the leader through the ACE approach if he is not already familiar with it. Explain what each lever of ACE means (mind, skill, body) and how the ACE model helps to align intent with impact. Provide specific examples of how ACE applies to him; for example, "The feedback here about coming off as if you are interrogating, transactional, and brusque is a function of the assumptions you're making about your role, the way you're engaging your audience, and your body language." Even using yourself as an example can go a long way.

2. Discuss what shifts he needs to make in each component of ACE to reach Signature Voice. Help him articulate what his baseline ACE is (revisit the drill at end of chapter 2) and what "future state" might look like. It can be helpful to lay these out in a From-To chart like the one shown in table 7-1. (You can also refer to the action plans

TABLE 7-1

Sample action plan for coaching

Conditioning areas	From . . .	To . . .
Assumptions (mental conditioning): What do I think and feel?	• My role is to get the information and data we need to solve the problem as quickly and efficiently as possible. • Only the end zone matters, let's move on to the next milestone.	• My role is to seek, absorb, and integrate information from others and build key relationships within the organization • The process for getting results is important, and it's worth my time to acknowledge interim wins for the team
Communication strategies (technical and skill conditioning): What do I say?	• Using advocacy as a dominant technique • Employing closed-ended questions to inquire • Providing feedback with an emphasis on "glass half-empty"	• Balancing communication with more listening, open-ended inquiry, and bridging • Providing feedback with an emphasis on "glass half full"
Energy (physical conditioning): How do I show up to others?	• Using a directive, brusque tone • Losing composure in conflict situations	• Managing tone according to the situation • Managing composure in conflict situations

for Terri and John in chapter 2 for additional examples.) We had one client say this was the single most helpful document he used throughout his development. He looked at it every day to remind himself what he aspired to in his drive for consistency and influence.

3. Help him determine concrete actions he can take in each area of conditioning. The more specific the action, the higher the chance he will act on it. For example, it is not enough to say "Be less interrogating." Instead, be precise about the change and how and where he might make it. For example, "Use open-ended questions versus closed-ended questions so it feels like less of an interrogation. When you disagree or have an alternate point of view, try asking a question instead of shooting down the point."

4. Encourage your direct report to continue to proactively seek additional input. Offer to support him in this way, if appropriate, and help him identify a few stakeholders in the organization who can give him periodic updates on what they observe about his presence as well.

Provide Trusted Advice

Once your direct report starts executing her action plan, it is common to encounter situations where she is unsure what to do or how to manage her presence. Most individuals need a sounding board at moments like these. As the manager, think of your role as guiding the individual to a solution rather than providing one. Walking your direct report through the situation using the quadrants and ACE to proactively plan is great preparation and can take a total of ten minutes. Here's what such a discussion might sound like:

Direct report: Hey, do you have a minute? I wanted to run my thoughts by you on the meeting I'm having later this week with the sales and marketing team.

Manager: Sure. I know we've talked about that group being a particularly important function for us to collaborate with.

Direct report: You know we're in a budget crunch. We haven't hit our revenue numbers so far this year, and going into the third quarter, the pressure is on to cut costs to improve the bottom line. I know that Joe, Tim, and their guys from sales and marketing are going to hit the roof when we discuss the rest of the year's forecast and proposed cuts at the meeting.

Manager: Tell me about your concerns.

Direct report: I'm concerned that it's going to turn into a shouting match rather than a discussion, especially if they start offering up excuses and wasting my time. We'll move away from the facts and the data and, as in the past, end up with both sides digging in their heels.

Manager: And?

Direct report: And that I'll end up impatient and annoyed. No doubt, I'll start questioning them in that interrogating way.

Manager: Losing voice for others and making that slide to driving voice.

Direct report: That's right. I need to figure out how to maintain my confidence and point of view without losing sight of the difficulties they're experiencing.

Manager: So the real question is, how do you ensure you stay in Signature Voice during the meeting and own the room?

Direct report: Right. It would be helpful to talk through ACE quickly.

Manager: Great, let me hear what you're thinking.

Direct report: For starters, I want to set the right tone for the meeting. Rather than going in with "I need that updated forecast to justify the cuts we're proposing," I want to go in with the assumption that I'm on the same side of the table with these guys. What are they experiencing out in the field? What's the impact on revenues? How can we *together* make the budget numbers? It would be great if I could propose a way forward while staying open to their thoughts. How can we together present to the executive team the best solution forward? In terms of communications, I think I need to frame the message around this intention, to state upfront that I'm here to understand their situation, propose a way forward, and jointly problem solve the budget issue.

At the same time, I don't want to abandon the data I have so far and my point of view that a budget cut will likely be warranted. If they're upset, I have to hear them out, and they may have some valid points in their pushback. For energy, I really need to watch the pace of my speech during this meeting and slow down if need be to maintain my composure. Maybe I could do a few of those breathing exercises right before to center myself.

Manager: Sounds like a plan to me. One additional thought if you want it. If possible, you may want to meet with Joe and Tim prior to the meeting just to feel them out and see where they are on this. They'd probably appreciate not being blindsided by your proposal.

Direct report: True. I'll see if I can get on their calendars before Tuesday.

Manager: If you want to do a run-through of the discussion prior to the meeting, give me a ring.

Acting as a sounding board doesn't require a huge investment of your time, but it can help your direct report work through concerns that he may not otherwise be able to. Sometimes just listening helps the individual to stop spinning out. Once the shared language and framework of presence is established, you can help the leader quickly diagnose and solve his own issues when he feels he's been triggered.

Celebrate Growth and Help Overcome Obstacles

Anyone who's picked up a new sport, instrument or started a new workout or weight-loss program knows the hardest part is sticking to it. Mastery of a skill or creating sustainable change requires regular practice. And it helps to be held accountable. Studies show that people who work out with a partner are much more likely to follow through on their commitments. While ACE provides a compelling way to think about and create an action plan for developing presence, the growth will only happen is if the leader applies the plan consistently over time. As manager, you can help provide some much-needed accountability. Do this by checking in, giving feedback about what you observe over time, and perhaps most importantly, letting him know when he's done something well. These small actions go a long way in helping the individual stay the course and make real progress.

A FINAL THOUGHT ON HELPING OTHERS FIND THEIR SIGNATURE VOICE

Working with leaders to find their Signature Voice is a responsibility and a privilege. It is a responsibility, in that once you tell someone what you and others see in their behavior, you must then help them reach their potential. It is a privilege because during the process, you become witness to a deep and personal passage on their leadership journey. And if you stay open, you are also given a tremendous learning opportunity along the way.

After having coached and trained so many leaders over the years, it would be easy for us to fall into the trap of thinking everyone falls into a certain pattern and provide cookie-cutter solutions. But recognizing that each person's journey to Signature Voice is an individual one, with its own nuances and peaks and valleys, we hold ourselves accountable to not drop into that rut. And as a result, we gain so much from each and every one of our clients. We learn something new every day about leadership presence and it never fails to amaze us how rich and powerful a leader's discovery of Signature Voice can be.

WHAT TO REMEMBER

- As a manager, you can use the Signature Voice framework to cultivate the talent on your team and support your direct reports' growth in presence.

- There are four ways to use the Signature Voice and ACE frameworks in your role as manager and coach:

  - *Offer a clear assessment of presence:* Help your direct reports understand how their presence is currently perceived and the impact it's having.

  - *Create an integrated action plan:* Help them articulate a plan to develop their presence using the ACE model.

  - *Offer coaching in real time:* Help them work through specific issues and challenges along the way

  - *Celebrate growth and help overcome obstacles:* Help them recognize the successes and obstacles that are part of the process.

CONCLUSION

I t has been a great honor for us to work with thousands of leaders on cultivating their Signature Voice. We are deeply grateful to all those who have shared their journeys with us—all of the hardworking clients whose stories went into this book. Everyone had a different story, but all shared in a struggle to understand what presence is and how to build it. Each eventually arrived at a place where they could be more authentic and connected as a leader, adapting to changing circumstances and new challenges, and ultimately, being more effective as a result of their diligence. They learned how to own the room.

As we worked on this book, the Summer Olympics were in the background. As we marveled at each of the athletes—whether competing in gymnastics, soccer, or swimming—we saw parallels between their aspirations and what it takes to build leadership presence. All the Olympians had come to the moment when their own unique mental, skill, and physical conditioning were tested. They had trained for years, fully committed to realizing their dreams. And, they had each done enough conditioning so that when the moment demanded—when they were finally competing for gold—their instincts, confidence, and presence took over. This is the same feeling leaders describe when they've owned and filled a room with a confident, clear leadership presence.

We've worked with executives in a variety of settings: in large classrooms, in small breakout groups during training programs, or in a leader's office over the course of a six-month coaching engagement. In each of those places, we hear over and over the pervasive myths about presence and how they threaten careers, promotions, and fulfillment. We see it as our work to continue to remove those obstacles so that these individuals can find their way. By doing that, we have uncovered a greater truth below the surface of each myth. At the start of this book, we shared three misconceptions regarding presence. Here, at the end of the book, we offer you a new way to consider each one.

Myth #1: You Are Who You Are

What's become clear over the years of working with leaders is that presence is not something you are born with or not. It is not an innate trait. Everyone has the human capacity to learn the two things that are essential to effective presence:

- To demonstrate one's value and distinctiveness (voice for self)

- To connect and align with others (voice for others)

When you tap into your Signature Voice, you are not finding a part of yourself that wasn't there before, you are becoming more of who you are. You become a whole leader, bringing more of your full self to work. Authenticity takes on a new meaning. You can differentiate between your true voice and the voice you developed out of habit or in reaction. The voice that you thought was the "real you" often turns out to be a hodgepodge of several things: who you thought you *should* be—who you were encouraged to be by well-meaning teachers and mentors—and the reactions that helped you over time to maintain an illusory sense of control. Through Signature Voice, you come to trust a deeper voice that holds personal conviction while maintaining respect for others. You may discover that you are "more you" than you were before.

John described himself as someone who enjoyed supporting others and felt most at ease when he was helping someone else. He realized over time that feels more like himself when he stands his ground and speaks his opinion while maintaining the natural compassion for others. He saw that helping someone else was often not a generous act, as he had told himself, but a need to control the situation or take on another person's feelings. Terri is more authentic when she can relax and deliver a direct message without judgment. She now allows herself to let go of the need to make people do what she wants them to. Instead, she takes charge in an appropriately respectful way. Terri is at her best when she is focused and calm and gives herself space to bring her "whole self" to the room.

Myth #2: One Size Fits All

Because Signature Voice is about becoming more of who you really are, then the one-size-fits-all approach doesn't work. We would never call this framework *Signature Voice* if we believed that homogeneity was the answer. Behaving or looking like someone else is a surefire way to chip away at your integrity and lose the respect of others. We created the ACE model to help leaders find the mental, skill, and physical conditioning that brings out their personal best. And it is different for everyone. The ultimate contribution a leader can make is to define her distinctive and authentic value proposition while taking ownership for the success of the organization.

Christine Day, the CEO of Lululemon Athletica, understands the importance of authenticity. In the past thirteen years, the apparel company has grown from a single yoga clothing store in Vancouver to largest yoga outfitter in the world, with 113 stores is the United States and Canada and over $700 million in annual sales. Day joined the company in 2008 after twenty years at Starbucks, where she started as Howard Schultz's assistant. The CEO is a regular yoga practitioner herself and credits the company's success with its strong ties to the yoga community.[1] Some describe the dedicated customers as a "cult following."[2] This has helped differentiate itself from larger competitors like Nike and Adidas. "If you want to be successful in this industry," she said in a *Fast Company* interview, "it's about being authentic."[3]

Myth #3: If It Ain't Broke, Don't Fix It

We often get calls from clients when challenges at work test their Signature Voice. Perhaps they are taking on a new role, or they have a CEO client who is particularly difficult, or their new team member is pushing their buttons. They're frustrated and say things like, "I thought I already worked through this" or "Why is this coming up now?" Leadership is dynamic, and therefore your presence needs to be as well. New bosses, new roles, and reorganizations are now part of everyday existence within organizations. Never before has business evolved at such a fast pace. For leaders to traverse this environment, they need to be both anchored and flexible, ready to adapt to whatever changes come their way. This means constantly and consistently working toward Signature Voice.

Howard Schultz is a good example of the tremendous power of tapping into your own authentic value proposition while adapting to the circumstance around them. From his days as a salesperson for Xerox to his renowned career with the Starbucks Company to ownership of the NBA Seattle SuperSonics, Schultz has demonstrated a capability to transition from one context to another evolving and growing as a leader along the way. In 2008, Schultz returned to his role at CEO of Starbucks after stepping away eight years earlier. He demonstrates all the substance of a leader who can set a clear vision, drive big initiatives, and set priorities while maintaining the style of a "beaming smile and empathetic tone," according to a 2011 *Fortune* magazine article.[4] His effective leadership has brought astounding results. By October 2011, Starbucks had reached revenues of $12 billion, profits of $1.7 billion, and with a reach of seventeen thousand retail stores, with a presence in every U.S. state and fifty-six countries.[5] Schultz's leadership presence reflects a powerful combination of substance and style.

We hope this book has inspired you to find your Signature Voice. If you are on the cusp of becoming a senior leader or officer in your organization, we hope that you find a way forward, recognizing the choices you have as a leader. You can do what has worked for you in the past, relying on the same tools in your toolbox. Or you can be conscious and intentional about your leadership presence, redefining your value proposition and shaping the opportunities ahead of you. It is a liberating moment when you turn off the autopilot, recognize you have a default position, and then realize you have a choice whether or not to go there. Finding your Signature Voice allows you to be the leader you want to be.

If you are a seasoned leader who has been operating in Signature Voice for some time, we hope you continue to strive for mastery and the self-fulfillment that comes along with it. That purpose will certainly guide you through the change that is inevitable in your role and organization. At those moments, we hope this book serves as a reminder to ask: What is my vision? Whom do I need to engage? How can my presence help lead me, and others, forward?

For the two of us, the journey continues as well. There were points in the writing of this book where our presence slid to our default positions, surfacing the creative (and at times difficult) tension that has existed in our business partnership since the beginning. At those moments we took our own advice and sought out ways to reset our assumptions, communicate more effectively, and manage our energy. That mind-skill-body conditioning helped to pull us out of conflict and return us to the authenticity in our message and the sense of purpose we both share in helping others enhance their presence. No leader is alone in struggles like these. As you continue your journey to Signature Voice, know that we are right there with you.

SIGNATURE VOICE TOOLKIT

W hen we work with coaching clients, we develop customized action plans to help them address their overall presence or prepare for specific situations where presence is critical. To help you create your own action plan, we offer a series of toolkits.

Depending on what your goal is, we've created three different toolkits to help you (table A-1)

TABLE A-1

If you...	Use this...	Description
Want to build your overall presence	Action Plan 1	Have you figured out which axis you need to strengthen but aren't sure where to start? Do you want to take your leadership presence to the next level? This toolkit takes you through a three-step process to assess your goals, identify the platform you should focus on, and strengthen your voice for self or voice for others.
Need to prepare for a specific meeting or event	Action Plan 2	Do you need a reminder of the ACE conditioning before you enter a high-stakes situation? This toolkit provides a series of checklists to help you prepare for any interaction that requires you to be in your Signature Voice.

(Continued)

TABLE A-1

(Continued)

If you...	Use this...	Description
Are facing a common leadership struggle	Action Plan 3	Are you up against a leadership challenge that is testing your presence? This toolkit provides sample coaching plans for addressing three of the most common leadership challenges: leading change, presenting to executive audiences, and influencing or negotiating with peers.

ACTION PLAN 1: BUILDING OVERALL EXECUTIVE PRESENCE

Have you figured out which axis you need to strengthen but aren't sure where to start? Do you want to take your leadership presence to the next level?

Step One

Refer to your ACE baseline at the end of chapter 2. What areas did you identify to work on? Fill out the worksheet below (table A-2) to organize the key issues you want to address.

TABLE A-2

Overall presence: Game plan

What impact do I want to have? _____

	My action plan
Assumptions: Mental conditioning	
Communication strategies: Skill conditioning	
Energy: Physical conditioning	

Step Two

Your presence manifests itself at three different levels of interactions: in one-on-one conversations, as a team or group leader, and as a representative of your organization. The skills and capabilities required against the ACE model differ against each of these platforms. Look at the chart below (figure A-1) and decide where it is most critical for you to develop your presence now. In the next step, you'll go deeper into one of these platforms.

Step Three

Once you have an idea of which kind of presence you would like to elevate, consider if an increase in voice for self or voice for

FIGURE A-1

ACE against different types of platforms

	Assumptions Mental conditioning: *What is my mind-set?*	Communication skills Skill conditioning: *What do I say?*	Energy Physical conditioning: *How am I showing up?*
One-to-one presence	❏ Aware of beliefs and assumptions about self, the other person, and the conversation	❏ Skilled in foundational listening and inquiry skills ❏ Skilled in foundational advocacy skills ❏ Skilled in influencing through effective framing and bridging	❏ Aware of impact and manages congruency of nonverbal communications
Group presence	❏ Aware of limiting or supportive assumptions about role in a group or team and impact ❏ Holds a cross-functional orientation; able to understand value and distinction of own and others' functions	❏ Able to communicate an agenda and vision for a team/group ❏ Able to negotiate boundaries and requests ❏ Able to cascade communications through teams ❏ Able to pull together varying agendas, secure buy-in, and coach	❏ Aware of and manages impact of own mood on team and group ❏ Proactively sets the tone for team and group
Organizational presence	❏ Has clarity in values, vision, and priorities; able to align those to the organization	❏ Skilled in communicating and framing vision, priorities, and agenda in context of organization ❏ Skilled in cascading communications at the enterprisewide level ❏ Skilled in messaging, sound bites, and storytelling in mobilizing others	❏ Understands importance of and responsibility for visibility and expanding sphere of influence ❏ Understands implications of executive endurance and sustainability

others would take your game to the next level. Find the action plan that best matches your situation and identify the behaviors you want to continue, do more of, and do less of.

The following pages offer action plans for each of these situations.

———————

Table A-3 highlights what to do if you'd like to *increase your voice for self in one-on-one interactions*. How can you leverage your strengths in voice for others when dealing with other individuals and what should you start or stop to enhance your voice for self?

Table A-4 highlights what to do if you'd like to *increase your voice for others in one-on-one interactions*. How can you leverage your strengths in voice for self when dealing with other individuals, and what should you start or stop to enhance your voice for others?

In most corporate environments today, individuals spend a majority of their time in meetings, representing their own agenda but that of their team and function as well. Therefore, group presence is critical.

Table A-5 highlights what to do if you'd like to *increase your voice for self in group settings*. How can you leverage your strengths in voice for self when representing your team or function and what should you start or stop to enhance your voice for others?

Table A-6 highlights what to do if you'd like to *increase your voice for others in group settings*. How can you leverage your strengths in voice for others when representing your team or function and what should you start or stop to enhance your voice for self?

As you move up in the organization and take on increasingly senior roles, you need to demonstrate presence at an enterprise level. It has an impact on multiple levels of people and your "wake" can either leave others inspired or drained. Table A-7

TABLE A-3

Presence: Increasing voice for self

Moving from supporting voice to Signature Voice

ACE drivers	Continue/strengths to leverage	Start/do more of	Stop/do less of
Assumptions: What assumptions do you have about yourself, the other person, and the interaction?	❑ Finding value in others and their contributions ❑ Placing importance on the relationship and people aspect	❑ Gaining clarity around your own needs, agenda, and values ❑ Valuing yourself as a peer to your peers and more senior stakeholders ❑ Articulating your value proposition—what you bring to the table	❑ Taking responsibility for and fearing other people's disapproval ❑ Believing that being respectful means being deferential
Communication strategies: What communication strategies or skills would help the interaction or relationship?	❑ Keeping ability to put self in others' shoes or lens ❑ Listening for the other person's agenda ❑ Asking questions ❑ Bridging to the other's concerns, needs, or language	❑ Adding more structure to how you speak or write ❑ Getting to the bottom line more quickly ❑ Offering a viewpoint and options sooner ❑ Making clearer requests	❑ Using apologetic, qualified, or self-effacing language ❑ Over-explaining the details and rationale ❑ Being the last to speak ❑ Listening as a way to avoid differences or confrontations
Energy: How are you showing up nonverbally to the other person?	❑ Demonstrating an open, friendly, and approachable demeanor	❑ Strengthening the pitch and volume of your voice ❑ Managing your composure to offset any signs of nervousness or anxiety ❑ Making sure your professional appearance reflects your leadership role	❑ Using nervous mannerisms such as inappropriate laughter or fidgety hand gestures ❑ Slouching or having an overeager posture or stance

TABLE A-4

Presence: Increasing voice for others

Moving from driving voice to Signature Voice

ACE drivers	Continue/strengths to leverage	Start/do more of	Stop/do less of
Assumptions: What assumptions do you have about yourself, the other person, and the interaction?	❑ Maintaining confidence in your viewpoint, conviction, and values ❑ Placing importance on achieving goals and objectives	❑ Thinking up front of the other person's issues, agenda, and style ❑ Having realistic expectations of others that align with their development or situation ❑ Demonstrating flexibility and picking your battles with discernment ❑ Seeking to understand first	❑ Thinking only of how you can benefit ❑ Expecting others to have the same or a higher level of competence or commitment than you do ❑ Assuming control/decision making in all situations ❑ Seeking to convince or be convinced first
Communication strategies: What communication strategies or skills would help the interaction or relationship?	❑ Speaking crisply and concisely ❑ Being direct and clear on the message itself ❑ Having a viewpoint and pathways forward	❑ Listening more ❑ Asking more questions to shape other's thinking ❑ Engaging others to a solution ❑ Telling stories that show your humility or empathy ❑ Explicitly communicating individual praise or acknowledgment	❑ Interrupting others ❑ Using advocacy (telling, directing) as your dominant communication technique ❑ Telling stories of your individual accomplishments ❑ Putting forth the solution or answer first
Energy: How are you showing up nonverbally to the other person?	❑ Demonstrating strength in the way you carry yourself	❑ Managing tone by situation ❑ Managing composure in conflict situations	❑ Using a directive, brusque, or harsh tone ❑ Showing agitation/frustration in tone and facial expressions

TABLE A-5

Group presence: Increasing voice for self

Moving from supporting voice to Signature Voice

ACE drivers	Continue/strengths to leverage	Start/do more of	Stop/do less of
Assumptions: What assumptions do you have about your division and other divisions?	□ Finding value in other divisions and their contributions □ Considering the impact of decisions on other divisions	□ Gaining clarity around your division's needs and agenda □ Valuing your division as one that brings critical value to other divisions □ Articulating the value proposition of your division □ Staying focused on key goals and objectives that drive results for the group	□ Discounting the impact of broad-based decisions on your own division □ Avoiding the politics of cross-functional dynamics □ Viewing organizational networking as a negative
Communication strategies: What communication strategies or skills would help your group presence?	□ Being able to articulate your appreciation for other divisions' agendas and contributions □ Being open to understanding others' boundaries, resources, and requests	□ Articulating your group's vision, agenda, and priorities □ Shaping and communicating key decisions with and for the group □ Managing and communicating your group's boundaries	□ Over-seeking the perspective of other divisions □ Being overly sensitive to the impact on other groups in decision making □ Saying "yes" to all requests from other groups, regardless of ownership
Energy: How are you showing up nonverbally to other groups?	□ Being aware of the mood of your group and other groups	□ Taking care of self and taking appropriate steps needed to recalibrate the tone/mood of the group	□ Being physically impacted by other divisions' requests and decisions □ Visibly taking on the negative mood of others

TABLE A-6

Group presence: Increasing voice for others

Moving from driving voice to Signature Voice

ACE drivers	Continue/strengths to leverage	Start/do more of	Stop/do less of
Assumptions: What assumptions do you have about your division and other divisions?	❑ Maintaining confidence in your division and your division's agenda ❑ Placing importance on achieving goals and objectives	❑ Thinking up front of other divisions' issues and agenda ❑ Having realistic expectations of other divisions that align with their agenda and priorities ❑ Demonstrating flexibility and picking your battles with discernment ❑ Seeking to understand first	❑ Thinking only of how your division can benefit ❑ Expecting other divisions to operate the same way as yours ❑ Assuming control/decision making in all situations ❑ Seeking to convince or be convinced first
Communication strategies: What communication strategies or skills would help your group presence?	❑ Speaking crisply and concisely ❑ Being direct and clear on the message itself ❑ Having a viewpoint and pathways forward	❑ Listening, acknowledging, and seeking perspective of other groups ❑ Considering the impact on others in decision making ❑ Pulling together the varying agendas and issues emanating from multiple stakeholder groups ❑ Enrolling stakeholders to secure buy-in for ideas and key decisions ❑ Delegating and coaching other group members	❑ Keeping other divisions out of the loop, information flow, or decision making ❑ Making repeated demands of other divisions without reciprocity ❑ Highlighting your group's accomplishments without giving or sharing credit with other groups ❑ Putting forth the solution as a singular effort or without gaining buy-in first
Energy: How are you showing up nonverbally to other groups?	❑ Demonstrating emotional and physical resilience and perseverance in times of adversity	❑ Managing composure in conflict situations with other divisions	❑ Expecting others to accept the mood you set with the group

Organizational presence: Increasing voice for self

Moving from supporting voice to Signature Voice

ACE drivers	Continue/strengths to leverage	Start/do more of	Stop/do less of
Assumptions: What assumptions do you have about your division and the enterprise?	❏ Considering the impact of decisions on the whole organization	❏ Acknowledging and articulating the value proposition you and your division bring to the broader organizational agenda ❏ Staying focused on key goals and objectives that move the needle and drive results for the organization	❏ Discounting the importance of what you and your team do in the context of the organizational agenda ❏ Getting tied up in "fire drills" and responding to all requests versus focusing on the organization's critical path
Communication strategies: What communication strategies or skills would help your organizational presence?	❏ Being able to engage multiple stakeholders for decision making	❏ Articulating the vision and priorities within and for the organization ❏ Challenging the organizational status quo when needed ❏ Using sound bites and messaging to convey clear, concise organizational priorities	❏ Minimizing your point of view ❏ "Spinning" or softening difficult news
Energy: How are you showing up nonverbally to the organization?	❏ Leveraging internal and external relationships/networks to support organizational mission	❏ Taking care of self and taking appropriate steps to endure organizational challenges ❏ Making requests of your network ❏ Managing your own energy	❏ Letting organizational stress impact your physical and emotional well-being ❏ Appearing frenzied or overwhelmed

TABLE A-8

Organizational presence: Increasing voice for others

Moving from driving voice to Signature Voice

ACE drivers	Continue/strengths to leverage	Start/do more of	Stop/do less of
Assumptions: What assumptions do you have about your division and the enterprise?	❑ Bringing passion and drive to the organizational agenda	❑ Thinking about the organizational agenda first over your divisional agenda ❑ Considering the broader context within which your division operates	❑ Thinking of and treating your division as different, separate, ahead of the pack, or more important than the rest of the enterprise ❑ Focusing on carving out or protecting your turf or territory ❑ Not valuing and understanding the role of all divisions—especially those that support the line businesses
Communication strategies: What communication strategies or skills would help your organizational presence?	❑ Being a strong organizational advocate internally and externally	❑ Using storytelling as a way to connect with organizational stakeholders ❑ Framing messages within the broader organizational context ❑ Cascading messages throughout the organization	❑ Communicating data, results, or agenda in a way that advocates for the division over what's best for the organization
Energy: How are you showing up nonverbally to the organization?	❑ Exuding confidence and command in times of crisis	❑ Mobilizing, focusing, and renewing the energy of those you lead by focusing on wins/strengths and not just gaps ❑ Owning the impact of your "ripple effect" and managing it	❑ Focusing only on senior-level relationships/networks ❑ Expecting the rest of the organization to have the same physical capacity for work as you

highlights what to do if you'd like to *increase your voice for self when representing your organization*. How can you leverage your strengths in voice for others and what should you start or stop to enhance your voice for self?

Table A-8 highlights what to do if you'd like to *increase your voice for others when representing your organization*. How can you leverage your strengths in voice for self, and what should you start or stop to enhance your voice for others?

ACTION PLAN 2: ACE PREPARATION CHECKLISTS

Are you about to enter a high-stakes situation and need a reminder of the ACE conditioning? In this section, we've included a set of checklists that serve as cues and reminders before you enter an important situation. Use these checklists to prepare yourself. They are easy to use and will save you time.

Step One: What's the Optimal ACE for the Situation?

For every situation, you need to decide what you want to achieve and what will work best for the given context, audience, and outcomes you desire. Use the worksheet in table A-9 to write down what you want to achieve for each element of ACE.

Step Two: Set the Right Assumptions

Often clients spend an inordinate amount of time on preparing slides or documents for meetings. What we've found is that just a bit of pregame planning to get in the right mind-set goes a long way.

Table A-10 is a checklist to help you set the assumptions that will help you be most effective in the given situation. It includes questions that focus your attention on voice for others (audience

TABLE A-9

ACE planning

What impact do I want to have in this situation? _____

	My game plan
Assumptions: Mental conditioning	
Communication strategies: Skill conditioning	
Energy: Physical conditioning	

TABLE A-10

Checklist 1: Assumptions about self and others

Focus	Assumptions checklist
Stakeholders	✓ *Who:* Who will be there? What are their roles? What is their preferred communication style? ✓ *Agenda:* What's in it for them? Why is this important to them? ✓ *Context:* What do they know?
My agenda	✓ *Key messages:* What is my point of view and recommendation? ✓ *Call to action:* What do I want the audience to do as a result of my message? ✓ *Impact:* What impression do I want to make on the audience?
My delivery	✓ *Opening:* How will I open the meeting/presentation? What will I say? ✓ *Questions:* How will I answer questions? ✓ *Options:* What alternative messages do I have in my back pocket? ✓ *Tone:* What is the tone I want to convey?

and stakeholders) and those that focus your attention on your voice for self (your message and delivery).

Step Three: Review Your Communications Repertoire

Now that you have a clear understanding of how you'll approach the meeting, consider the communications repertoire available to you. How will you frame this meeting? How will you ensure your message is crisp and concise? How will you engage the audience? How will you listen and ask questions to ensure it's a two-way dialogue?

On the following pages are three checklists (tables A-11, A-12, A-13) that serve as quick and easy reminders of communication

TABLE A-11

Checklist 2: Framing

Do's	Don'ts
Frame:	*Frame:*
✓ Offer the other person a new way of seeing the situation or process	✗ Provide details without providing context
✓ Simplify the complexity by boiling it down to a few key issues (e.g., "It sounds like there are three things that will make this project successful . . .")	✗ Free associate without structures
✓ Structure your communications with headlines first, then details	

TABLE A-12

Checklist 3: Structured advocacy

Do's	Don'ts
Message:	*Message:*
✓ Get to the core of what you are trying to say or request	✗ Do it last-minute or on the fly
✓ Spend time to prepare, if possible	✗ Bog the receiver down in process-oriented detail
✓ Focus on results and outcomes	✗ Have no structure in your communication
✓ Ground in compelling evidence	✗ Explain the details of your decision-making process
✓ Use structure	
Audience:	*Audience:*
✓ Consider their communication style	✗ Use a cookie-cutter approach for all people
✓ Put yourself in his/her shoes	✗ Assume they know the context
✓ Find what's in it for them	✗ Miss their key need or opportunity

TABLE A-13

Checklist 4: Listening and asking questions

Do's	Don'ts
Listening:	*Listening:*
✓ Allow time and space for answers	✗ Provide details without providing context
✓ Summarize content	✗ Free associate without structure
✓ Be tuned into underlying emotions or motivations	✗ Interrupt
	✗ Process your response while the other party is speaking
Asking questions:	*Asking questions:*
✓ Use responses to shape the discussion	✗ Ask closed-ended questions
✓ Use "what" or "how" questions	✗ Ask multiple questions at a time
✓ Test assumptions	✗ Overuse "why" questions
✓ Build on what has already been said	

skills do's and don'ts. Remember to use all three skills in concert with each other, using each as it's called for.

Step Four: Manage Your Energy

Carl W. Buechner once said, "They may forget what you said, but they will never forget how you made them feel." Don't let all of your preparation around assumptions and communication skills go to waste because you've failed to manage your energy.

Instead, you need to observe and manage your nonverbal cues against each of the six cue points so they are congruent to what you are thinking and saying. After all, nothing erodes presence more than sending a message with your body language that is out of alignment with the message you are communicating verbally.

Remember the importance of authenticity. Table A-14 is a checklist of nonverbal do's and don'ts. We don't prescribe a one-size-fits-all approach to body language but we find that certain behaviors always serve as detractors while others, if done authentically, can enhance your presence.

TABLE A-14

CENTER: Nonverbal do's and don'ts

Context	Do's	Don'ts
Core posture	✓ Hold head up straight and relaxed ✓ Lead your posture from the chest/heart rather than the neck or hip	✗ Slouch ✗ Hold yourself tense with shoulders raised ✗ Stand/sit with your hip cocked to the side
Eye contact	✓ Make direct eye contact when speaking (adjust for culture)	✗ Always look upward, sideways, or down while speaking (adjust for culture)
Natural gestures	✓ Use gestures to help make your point ✓ Manage your gestures by anchoring them either at the side of your body (if standing) or on the table/chair arms (if sitting)	✗ Continuously touch your face or hair ✗ Use nervous, fidgety mannerisms, such as clicking a pen or playing with a paper clip
Tone, tempo, timing	✓ Pace yourself by pausing at natural points, such as end of sentences, or transitions ✓ Calibrate your tone to the situation, person, and delivery mode	✗ Use "up-speak" in your tempo ✗ Speak too quickly ✗ Use an overly composed or overly expressive tone
Expressions of the face	✓ Look engaged and interested in the content and questions	✗ Show visible frustration or annoyance by frowning, rolling your eyes, etc.
Regions plus territories	✓ In group settings, situate yourself close to others versus away from the table or group ✓ When speaking to someone, stand a few feet apart	✗ Withdraw from the rest of the group by sitting/standing at a distance ✗ Stand too close or too far from someone when speaking to them

ACTION PLAN 3: SAMPLE ACE PLANS FOR COMMON LEADERSHIP SITUATIONS

Are you up against a leadership challenge that is testing your presence? This section provides sample ACE plans for addressing three of the most common leadership challenges:

- Leading change
- Presenting to executive audiences
- Influencing or negotiating with peers

Use these plans as a starting point to develop your own action plan.

ACE FOR LEADING CHANGE

Change is no longer episodic. It is a now a given. All leaders need to know how to lead change initiatives, help with reorganizations, and communicate new policies and decisions that impact others' lives and the organizations on a daily basis.

Figure A-2 is an illustrative ACE plan for an individual who needs to demonstrate presence during a particularly challenging change.

ACE FOR PRESENTING TO EXECUTIVE AUDIENCES

Whether you are an executive or an aspiring one, presenting to an executive audience can be a high-stakes situation. You often have little time to make your point, demonstrate thought leadership, and get the approval or buy-in you need.

Figure A-3 is a sample ACE action plan for an individual who needs to communicate, formally or informally, with an executive audience.

ACE FOR INFLUENCING PEERS

In today's increasingly cross-functional, matrixed, and global organization, the ability to influence without direct authority has become a prerequisite for leadership. Our presence, especially with peers in other areas, can make or break projects and initiatives. Figure A-4 is a sample action plan for an individual who needs to influence or negotiate with peers.

Illustrative ACE plan for leading change

What impact do I want to have?

Authentic and connected

	Action steps
Assumptions: Mental conditioning	☐ Find your own reason to believe first. ☐ Assume people will experience grief and denial at an "ending" and need acknowledgment of their experience. ☐ Be prepared for resistance—it's natural.
Communication strategies: Skill conditioning	☐ Acknowledge the challenge or loss. ☐ Frame the change in a bigger picture; tie to "uber-goals" and strategic priorities. ☐ Paint a way forward and provide vision. ☐ Make an offer to stay in dialogue.
Energy: Physical conditioning	☐ Demonstrate composure in the face of denial and resistance. ☐ When others are "spinning," continually bring them to the bigger picture and perspectives as to why what is happening is important. ☐ Set a tone that allows for open dialogue, helping folks to explore and take hold of a new way forward.

"No doubt we're in a challenging environment, a new paradigm. An era has ended and we've done good work against that."

"Here are the reasons I/we believe this is important."

"Here's what I see ahead for us. I encourage all of us to stay open and in dialogue around how we can move forward together."

Illustrative ACE plan for presenting to executive audiences

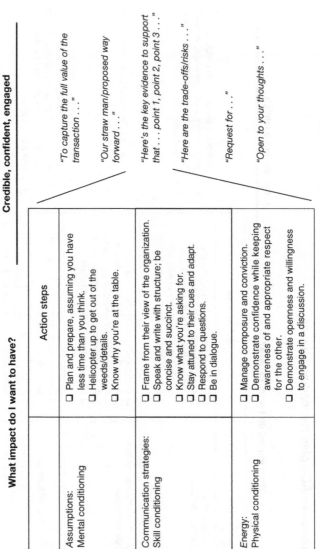

What impact do I want to have?

Credible, confident, engaged

Action steps

Assumptions:
Mental conditioning

☐ Plan and prepare, assuming you have less time than you think.
☐ Helicopter up to get out of the weeds/details.
☐ Know why you're at the table.

"To capture the full value of the transaction . . ."

"Our straw man/proposed way forward . . ."

Communication strategies:
Skill conditioning

☐ Frame from their view of the organization.
☐ Speak and write with structure; be concise and succinct.
☐ Know what you're asking for.
☐ Stay attuned to their cues and adapt.
☐ Respond to questions.
☐ Be in dialogue.

"Here's the key evidence to support that . . . point 1, point 2, point 3 . . ."

"Here are the trade-offs/risks . . ."

Energy:
Physical conditioning

☐ Manage composure and conviction.
☐ Demonstrate confidence while keeping awareness of and appropriate respect for the other.
☐ Demonstrate openness and willingness to engage in a discussion.

"Request for . . ."

"Open to your thoughts . . ."

Illustrative ACE plan for influencing/negotiating with peers

What impact do I want to have?

Clear and respectful

	Action steps	
Assumptions: Mental conditioning	☐ Stay objective; don't take things personally. ☐ Focus on the shared enterprise or company goal or priority that offers common ground. ☐ Negotiate on decision-making criteria to get to the best decision versus arguing positions.	"Given the decision made to assess risk for the project, I wanted to meet to discuss how we could meet this objective and the aggressive two-week deadline on this . . ." "Would be great to understand your team's priorities against this and share my situation . . ."
Communication strategies: Skill conditioning	☐ Frame with the shared goal and how to problem solve this together. ☐ Listen and inquire to understand differing viewpoints. ☐ Reframe, bridge, or connect your point of view to what you heard; uncover and share all assumptions at play. ☐ Get to mutual understanding of the situation. ☐ Seek to jointly problem solve. ☐ Make a direct request for or offer suggestions for future action.	"What conditions could we brainstorm to meet your need around x and my need around y . . ." "To recap so far, we share common views around x and the problem we need to solve for is y . . ."
Energy: Physical conditioning	☐ Demonstrate appropriate confidence and respect, even to differing opinions.	"Here's a proposed next step . . . what do you think?"

NOTES

INTRODUCTION

1. Belle Linda Halpern and Kathy Lubar, *Leadership Presence: Dramatic Techniques to Reach Out, Motivate, and Inspire* (New York: Gotham, 2003).

2. Harrison Monarth, *Executive Presence: The Art of Commanding Respect Like a CEO* (New York: McGraw-Hill, 2010).

3. D. A. Benton, *Executive Charisma: Six Steps to Mastering the Art of Leadership* (New York: McGraw-Hill, 2003).

CHAPTER ONE

1. Catalyst Inc., *The Double-Bind Dilemma for Women in Leadership: Damned If You Do, Doomed If You Don't*, July 2007, http://www.catalyst.org/publication/83/the-double-bind-dilemma-for-women-in-leadership-damned-if-you-do-doomed-if-you-dont.

2. Norihiko Shirouzo and Mariko Sanchanta, "Support for Leadership Wavers at Auto Giant: While Top Management Backs President Akio Toyoda, Middle Managers and Rank-and-File Express Doubts Amid Crisis," *Wall Street Journal*, February 24, 2010.

3. Micheline Maynard, "3 Hard Lessons Akio Toyoda Learned From Toyota's Debacle," *Forbes.com*, June 13, 2012.

CHAPTER TWO

1. Lori Montgomery and Yolanda Woodlee, "It's Official: Williams Endorses Cropp," *Washington Post*, May 17, 2006.

2. Lori Montgomery, "In Sweep, Fenty Draws on Uniting to Conquer," *Washington Post*, September 14, 2006.

3. David Nakamura, "Cropp and Fenty Have Pursued Their Legislative Agendas by Opposite Means," *Washington Post*, August 21, 2006.

4. Alan Suderman, "Is Adrian Fenty a Jerk?" *Washington City Paper*, August 20, 2010.

5. Nsenga Burton, "D.C. Mayor Fenty Apologizes for 'Aloof Manage-ment Style,'" *The Root*, September 3, 2010.

6. Jonathan Mummolo and Nikita Stewart, "Missteps in Crash's After-math Dull Fenty's Luster," *Washington Post*, July 3, 2009.

7. Nikita Stewart and Paul Schwartzman, "How Adrian Fenty Lost His Reelection Bid for D.C. Mayor," *Washington Post*, September 16, 2010.

8. Ibid.

CHAPTER THREE

1. See the following:

Daniel Goleman, "Research Affirms Power of Positive Thinking," *New York Times*, February 3, 1987.

Hans Villarica, "How the Power of Positive Thinking Won Scien-tific Credibility," *The Atlantic.com*, April 23, 2012, http://www .theatlantic.com/health/archive/2012/04/how-the-power-of-positive-thinking-won-scientific-credibility/256223/.

Sharon Jayson, "Power of a Super Attitude," *USA Today*, Octo-ber 4, 2004.

2. Associated Press, "Yang Ensures Major-less Year for Tiger," Au-gust 17, 2009, http://sports.espn.go.com/golf/pgachampionship09/news/story?id=4403199; Larry Dorman, "Y.E. Yang Shocks Woods to Win at P.G.A.," *The New York Times*, August 16, 2009.

3. Associated Press, "Yang Ensures Major-less Year for Tiger."

4. Tom Rath, *StrengthsFinder 2.0* (New York: Gallup Press, 2007).

5. Video of NIH All-Hands Town Meeting with Francis Collins, August 2009, http://videocast.nih.gov/summary.asp?file=15247.

6. Ram Charan, Stephen Drotter, and James Noel, *The Leadership Pipeline: How to Build the Leadership-Powered Company* (San Francisco: Jossey-Bass, 2000), 67.

7. William Ury, *Getting Past No: Negotiating Your Way from Confron-tation to Cooperation*, (New York: Bantam Books, 1991), 19.

8. Leigh Steinberg and Michael D'Orso, *Winning with Integrity: Get-ting What You're Worth Without Selling Your Soul* (New York: Villard, 1998), 62, 67.

9. Ronald A. Heifetz, Marty Linksy, and Alexander Grashow, *The Practice of Adaptive Leadership: Tools and Tactics for Changing Your Organization and the World* (Boston: Harvard Business Press, 2009).

CHAPTER FOUR

1. Adam Bryant, "A Blueprint for Leadership: Show, Don't Tell," *New York Times*, December 10, 2011.

2. Question-and-answer session with Microsoft CEO Steve Ballmer and students of the Stanford University Business School, Stanford, California, March 15, 2007, http://www.microsoft.com/en-us/news/exec/steve/2007/03-15stanford.aspx.

CHAPTER FIVE

1. See, for example: Albert Mehrabian. *Silent Messages: Implicit Communication of Emotions and Attitudes*, 2nd ed. (Stamford: Wadsworth Publishing Company, 1981).

2. Roy Baumeister and Ellen Bratslavsky, "Bad Is Stronger Than Good," *Review of General Psychology* 5, no. 4 (2001): 323-370.

3. Rob Cross, Wayne Baker, and Andrew Parker, "What Creates Energy in Organizations?" *MIT Sloan Management Review*, July 15, 2003.

4. Michael Campbell, et. al. "The Stress of Leadership," Center for Creative Leadership, 2007, http://www.ccl.org/leadership/pdf/research/StressofLeadership.pdf.

5. Jim Loehr and Tony Schwartz, *The Power of Full Engagement* (New York: Free Press, 2004), 28, 48.

6. Daniel Goleman, Annie McKee, and Richard Boyatzis, *Primal Leadership: Learning to Lead with Emotional Intelligence* (Boston: Harvard Business School Press, 2002), 5, 18.

7. Kayla Webley, "How the Nixon-Kennedy Debate Changed the World," *Time*, September 23, 2010.

8. Kevin Van Valkenburg and Rick Maese, "From Baltimore to Beijing: Does Music Give Phelps an Unfair Advantage?" *Baltimore Sun*, August 13, 2008.

9. Frank Deford, "The Ring Leader," *Sports Illustrated*, May 10, 1999.

10. "Michael Jordan," *NBA Encyclopedia—Playoff Edition*, http://www.nba.com/history/players/jordan_bio.html.

11. Herminia Ibarra and Mark Hunter, "How Leaders Create and Use Network," *Harvard Business Review*, January 2007.

12. Ibid.

CHAPTER SIX

1. William B. Joiner and Stephen A. Josephs, *Leadership Agility: Five Levels of Mastery for Anticipating and Initiating Change* (San Francisco: Jossey-Bass, 2006).

2. CNBC interview, "Warren Buffett: The Billionaire Next Door," March 1, 2007, http://www.cnbc.com/id/17401056/site/14081545/.

3. Melissa J. Anderson, "Voice of Experience: Rhonda Mims, President, ING Foundation & SVP, Corporate Responsibility and Multicultural Affairs, ING," *The Glass Hammer*, January 13, 2011, http://www.theglasshammer.com/news/2011/01/13/voice-of-experience-rhonda-mims-president-ing-foundation-svp-corporate-responsibility-and-multicultural-affairs-ing/.

CONCLUSION

1. "2011 Businessperson of the Year," *Fortune*, November 17, 2011.

2. Danielle Sacks, "Lululemon's Cult of Selling," *Fast Company*, April 14, 2009.

3. Ibid.

4. David A. Kaplan, "Strong Coffee," *Fortune Magazine*, December 12, 2011.

5. Ibid.

INDEX

ABOUT THE AUTHORS

AMY JEN SU and MURIEL MAIGNAN WILKINS are executive coaches and leadership development consultants who have served clients in a variety of industries including biotechnology, financial services, management consulting, private equity, and nonprofits. They are cofounders and managing partners of Isis Associates, a boutique leadership coaching and consulting firm, with offices in Washington, DC and Boston. They have worked with thousands of high-potential and senior leaders through their Signature Voice™ training and coaching program. Known for their business know-how and executive development expertise, they are sought-after speakers on the subject of leadership presence and facilitators for transformative leadership development programs. They are co-contributors to a *Harvard Business Review* blog.

Amy Jen Su has a degree in psychology from Stanford University and an MBA from Harvard Business School. She is known for helping leaders authentically build vision, voice, and followership. Her previous experience includes advising senior executives as a management consultant for Booz Allen & Hamilton and working as a strategic planner for Taco Bell. Her expertise as a certified Integral coach and certified teacher of yoga and meditation have given her a uniquely sustainable and transformational approach to leadership development.

Muriel Maignan Wilkins holds an MBA from Harvard Business School and a BS in marketing and international business from Georgetown University. Previously, she held advisory and leadership roles in marketing and strategy at Prudential, Accenture, and *U.S. News & World Report*. She has a strong track record of helping leaders develop in the critical impact areas of executive presence, role transitions, and relationship management. Deeply influenced by nearly twenty years of living in North Africa, Europe, and the Caribbean, she brings a valued global perspective to her work as a leadership consultant.